W9-AAI-329

Evidence-Based Instruction in Reading

A Professional Development Guide to Phonics

Evidence-Based Instruction in Reading

A Professional Development Guide to Phonics

Belinda S. Zimmerman

Kent State University and *Kent City Schools*

Nancy D. Padak

Kent State University

Timothy V. Rasinski

Kent State University

Boston • New York • San Francisco
Mexico City • Montreal • Toronto • London • Madrid • Munich • Paris
Hong Kong • Singapore • Tokyo • Cape Town • Sydney

Executive Editor: *Aurora Martínez Ramos*
Series Editorial Assistant: *Lynda Giles*
Director of Professional Development: *Alison Maloney*
Marketing Manager: *Danae April*
Production Editor: *Gregory Erb*
Editorial Production Service: *Publishers' Design and Production Services, Inc.*
Composition Buyer: *Linda Cox*
Manufacturing Buyer: *Linda Morris*
Electronic Composition: *Publishers' Design and Production Services, Inc.*
Interior Design: *Publishers' Design and Production Services, Inc.*
Cover Designer: *Kristina Mose-Libon*

For related titles and support materials, visit our online catalog at
www.ablongman.com.

Copyright © 2008 Pearson Education, Inc.

All rights reserved. No part of the material protected by this copyright notice may
be reproduced or utilized in any form or by any means, electronic or mechanical,
including photocopying, recording, or by any information storage and retrieval system, without written permission from the copyright owner.

To obtain permission(s) to use material from this work, please submit a written
request to Allyn and Bacon, Permissions Department, 75 Arlington Street, Boston,
MA 02116 or fax your request to 617-848-7320.

Between the time website information is gathered and then published, it is not
unusual for some sites to have closed. Also, the transcription of URLs can result in
typographical errors. The publisher would appreciate notification where these
errors occur so that they may be corrected in subsequent editions.

Library of Congress Cataloging-in-Publication Data

Zimmerman, Belinda S.
  Evidence-based instruction in reading : a professional development guide
to phonics / Belinda S. Zimmerman, Nancy D. Padak, Timothy V. Rasinski.
      p.   cm.
  Includes bibliographical references and index.
  ISBN-13: 978-0-205-45630-7 (alk. paper)
  ISBN-10: 0-205-45630-8 (alk. paper)
    1. Reading--Phonetic method—United States.   2. Reading
teachers—In-service training—United States.   I. Padak, Nancy.   II.
Rasinski, Timothy V.   III. Title.   IV. Title: Professional development guide
to phonics.

  LB1050.34.Z56 2008
  372.46'5—dc22

                                                                2007044068

Printed in the United States of America

10 9 8 7 6 5 4 3 2 1   RRD-VA   11 10 09 08 07

Photo Credits: pp. 1, 15, 67: Lindfors Photography; p. 43: Bob Daemmrich
Photography; p. 55: IndexOpen

Among us, we have been teachers and teacher educators for nearly 100 years! During this time, we have developed deep and abiding respect for teachers and trust in their ability to offer their students the very best possible instruction. Yet we also agree with librarian John Cotton Dana (1856–1929), who said, "Who dares to teach must never cease to learn."

Our careers have been marked by continual learning. We dedicate this book to all who have taught us and all whom we have taught— all who have dared to teach.

NP
TR
MM
EN
BZ

About the Authors

Belinda S. Zimmerman is an adjunct Professor of Education at Kent State University where she teaches graduate and undergraduate courses in literacy education. In addition to years of experience as a classroom teacher, she is a professional development coordinator, a trained Reading Recovery teacher, a literacy specialist, a literacy coach, and co-director of a mentorship program for entry-year teachers. Dr. Zimmerman also serves as a Regional Literacy Consultant for the Ohio Department of Education. Her interests related to literacy are many, but she has always focused on helping struggling readers to achieve success and in assisting teachers in providing the highest quality literacy instruction possible for all learners. She is co-author of the book *Phonics Poetry*, which she wrote with Dr. Timothy Rasinski. She holds a bachelor's degree in elementary education and a master's degree in reading specialization. Dr. Zimmerman earned her PhD from Kent State University with the leadership and support of Dr. Nancy Padak and Dr. Timothy Rasinski.

Nancy D. Padak is a Distinguished Professor of Education at Kent State University where she directs the Reading and Writing Center and teaches graduate courses in literacy education and recently received the honor of Kent State University Distinguished Professor. She was a part of the team that wrote the initial grant to fund the state literacy resource center at Kent State University–Ohio Literacy Resource Center (OLRC) and has been a middle school and high school classroom teacher and administrator in a large urban school district. She frequently works with teachers and has written or edited a dozen books and more than 100 scholarly articles. Professor Padak is a past College Reading Association President and a former editor of *The Reading Teacher*. She currently edits the *Journal of Literacy Research*.

Timothy V. Rasinski is a Professor of Education in the Department of Teaching, Leadership, and Curriculum Studies at Kent

State University. He teaches graduate and undergraduate courses in literacy education. His major interests include working with children who find reading difficult, phonics and reading fluency instruction, and teacher development in literacy education. He has published over 100 articles and 10 books on various aspects of reading education. Dr. Rasinski is past editor of *The Reading Teacher* and is currently an editor for the *Journal of Literacy Research*. He has served as president of the College Reading Association and on the Board of Directors of the International Reading Association. He earned bachelor's degrees in economics and education at the University of Akron and the University of Nebraska at Omaha. His master's degree in special education also comes from the University of Nebraska at Omaha. Dr. Rasinski was awarded the PhD from The Ohio State University.

Contents

Series Introduction

Evidence-Based Instruction in Reading: A Professional Development Guide

Better than a thousand days of diligent study is one day spent with a great teacher.

JAPANESE PROVERB

*L*earning to read is perhaps a young child's greatest school accomplishment. Of course, reading is the foundation for success in all other school subjects. Reading is critical to a person's intellectual development, later economic success, and the pleasure that is to be found in life.

Similarly, teaching a child to read is one of the greatest accomplishments a teacher can ever hope for. And yet, reading and teaching reading are incredibly complex activities. The reading process involves elements of a person's psychological, physical, linguistic, cognitive, emotional, and social world. Teaching reading, of course, involves all these and more. Teachers must orchestrate the individuality of each child they encounter; the physical layout of the classroom and attendant materials; their own colleagues, parents, and the school administration; the school's specified curriculum; and their own style of teaching! The popular cliché that "teaching reading is not rocket science" perhaps underestimates the enormity of the task of teaching children to read.

The complexity of teaching reading can be, quite simply, overwhelming. How does a teacher teach and find mastery of the various skills in reading, attend to the school and state curricular guidelines, and use an appropriate variety of materials, while simultaneously meeting the individual needs of all children in the classroom? We think that it was because of the enormous complexity of this task that many teachers resorted to prepackaged reading programs to provide the structure and sequence for a given grade level. Basal reading programs, for example, provide some assurance that at least some of the key skills and content for reading are covered within a given period of time.

The problem with prepackaged programs is that they are not sensitive to the culture of the classroom, school, and community; the individual children in the classroom; and the instructional style of the teacher. The one-size-fits-all approach adopted by such programs—with, of course, the best of intentions—resulted in programs that met the minimal needs of the students, that lacked the creative flair that only a teacher can give a program, and that absolved teachers of a good deal of the accountability for teaching their students. If children failed to learn to read, it was the fault of the program.

The fact of the matter is that many children failed to learn to read up to expectations using prepackaged programs. The results of periodic assessments of U.S. students' reading achievement, most notably the National Assessment of Educational Progress, have demonstrated little, if any, growth in student reading achievement over the past 30 years. This lack of growth in literacy achievement is at least partially responsible for equally dismal results in student growth in other subject areas that depend highly on a student's ability to read.

The National Reading Panel Report

Having noticed this disturbing trend, the National Reading Panel (NRP) was formed by the United States Congress in 1996 and given the mandate of reviewing the scientific research related to reading and determining those areas that science has shown have the greatest promise for improving reading achievement in the elementary grades. In 2000, the NRP came out with its findings. Essentially, the panel found that the existing scientific research points to five particular areas of reading that have the greatest promise of increasing reading achievement: phonemic awareness, phonics and word decoding, reading fluency, vocabulary, and reading comprehension. Additionally, the NRP indicated that investments in teachers, through professional development activities, hold promise of improving student reading achievement.

The findings of the NRP have been the source of considerable controversy, yet they have been used by the federal and state governments, as well as local school systems, to define and mandate reading instruction. In particular, the federal Reading First program has mandated that any school receiving funds from Reading First must embed within its reading curriculum direct and systematic teaching of phonemic awareness, phonics, reading fluency, vocabulary, and comprehension. The intent of the mandate, of course, is to provide students with the instruction that is based on best evidence that it will have a positive impact on students' reading achievement.

Although we may argue about certain aspects of the findings of the National Reading Panel, in particular what it left out of its report of effective instructional principles, we find ourselves in solid agreement with the panel that the five elements that it identified are indeed critical to success in learning to read.

Phonemic awareness is crucial to early reading development. Students must develop an ability to think about the sounds of language and to manipulate those sounds in various ways—to blend sounds, to segment words into sounds, and so on. An inability to deal with language sounds in this way will set the stage for difficulty in phonics and word decoding. To sound out a word, which is essentially what phonics requires of students, readers must have adequate phonemic awareness. Yet, some estimates indicate that as many as 20 percent of young children in the United States do not have sufficient phonemic awareness to profit fully from phonics instruction.

Phonics, or the ability to decode written words in text, is clearly essential for reading. Students who are unable to accurately decode at least 90 percent of the words they encounter while reading will have difficulty gaining appropriate meaning from what they read. We prefer to expand the notion of phonics to word decoding. Phonics, or using the sound–symbol relationship between letters and words, is, without doubt, an important way to solve the problem of unknown words. However, there are other methods to decode written words. These include attending to the prefixes, suffixes, and base elements of longer words; examining words for rimes (word families) and other letter patterns; using meaningful context to determine unknown words; dividing longer words into smaller parts through syllabication; and making words part of one's sight vocabulary, words recognized instantly and by sight. Good readers are able to employ all of these strategies and more. Appropriately, instruction needs to be aimed at helping students develop proficiency in learning to decode words using multiple strategies.

Reading fluency refers to the ability to read words quickly, as well as accurately, and with appropriate phrasing and expression. Fluent readers are able to decode words so effortlessly that they can direct their cognitive resources away from the low-level decoding task to the more important meaning-making or comprehension part of reading. For a long time, fluency was a relatively neglected area of the reading curriculum. In recent years, however, educators have realized that although fluency deals with the ability to efficiently and effortlessly decode words, it is also critical to good reading comprehension and needs to be part of any effective reading curriculum.

Word and concept meaning is the realm of *vocabulary*. Not only must readers be able to decode or sound out words but they must also know what these words mean. Instruction aimed at expanding students' repertoire of word meanings and deepening their understanding of already known words is essential to reading success. Thus, vocabulary instruction is an integral part of an effective instructional program in reading.

Accurate and fluent decoding of words, coupled with knowledge of word meanings, may seem to ensure *comprehension*. However, there is more to it than that. Good readers also actively engage in constructing meaning, beyond individual words, from what they read. That is, they engage in meaning-constructing strategies while they read. These include ensuring that they employ their background knowledge for the topics they encounter in reading. It also means that they ask questions, make predictions, and create mental images while they read. Additionally, readers monitor their reading comprehension and know when to stop and check things out when things begin to go awry—that is, when readers become aware that they are not making adequate sense out of what they are reading. These are just some of the comprehension strategies and processes good readers use while they read to ensure that they understand written texts. These same strategies must be introduced and taught to students in an effective reading instruction program.

Phonemic awareness, phonics/decoding, reading fluency, vocabulary, and comprehension are the five essential elements of effective reading programs identified by the National Reading Panel. We strongly agree with the findings of the NRP—these elements must be taught to students in their reading program.

Rather than get into in-depth detail on research and theory related to these topics, our intent in this series is to provide you with a collection of simple, practical, and relatively easy-to-implement instructional strategies, proven through research and actual practice, for teaching each of the five essential components. We think you will find the books in this series readable and practical. Our hope is that you will use these books as a set of handbooks for developing more effective and engaging reading instruction for all your students.

Professional Development in Literacy

Effective literacy instruction requires teachers to be knowledgeable, informed professionals capable of assessing student needs and responding to those needs with an assortment of instructional strategies. Whether you are new to the field or a classroom veteran, ongoing professional development is imperative. Professional development influences instructional practices which, in turn, affect student achievement (Wenglinsky, 2000). Effective professional development is not simply an isolated program or activity; rather it is an ongoing, consistent learning effort where links between theoretical knowledge and the application of that knowledge to daily classroom practices are forged in consistent and meaningful ways (Renyi, 1998).

Researchers have noted several characteristics of effective professional development: It must be grounded in research-based practices; it must be collaborative, allowing teachers ample opportunities to share knowledge, as well as teaching and learning challenges, among colleagues; and it must actively engage teachers in assessing, observing, and responding to the learning and development of their students (Darling-Hammond & McLaughlin, 1995). This professional development series, *Evidence-Based Instruction in Reading: A Professional Development Guide*, is intended to provide a roadmap for systematic, participatory professional development initiatives.

Using the Books

The *Evidence-Based Instruction in Reading* series consists of five professional development books, each addressing one major component of literacy instruction identified by the National Reading Panel (2000) and widely accepted in the field as necessary for effective literacy programs: phonemic awareness, phonics, vocabulary, fluency, and comprehension. These five components are not, by any means, the only components needed for effective literacy instruction. Access to appropriate reading materials, productive home–school connections, and a desire to learn to read and write are also critical pieces of the literacy puzzle. It is our hope, however, that by focusing in depth on each of the five major literacy components, we can provide educators and professional development facilitators with concrete guidelines and suggestions for enhancing literacy instruction. Our hope is that teachers who read, reflect, and act on the information in these books will be more able to provide effective instruction in each of the five essential areas of reading.

Each book is intended to be used by professional development facilitators, be they administrators, literacy coaches, reading specialists, and/or classroom teachers, and program participants as they engage in professional development initiatives or in-service programs within schools or school districts. The use of the series can be adapted to meet the specific needs and goals of a group of educators. For example, a school may choose to hold a series of professional development sessions on each of the five major components of literacy instruction; it may choose to focus in depth on one or two components that are most relevant to its literacy program; or it may choose to focus on specific aspects, such as assessment or instructional strategies, of one or more of the five areas.

The books may also be useful in professional book club settings. An icon, included at spots for book club discussion, marks times when you might wish to share decisions about your own classroom to get colleagues' feedback. You might also want to discuss issues or solve problems with colleagues. Appendix A lists several other possible book club activities. These are listed by chapter and offer opportunities to delve into issues mentioned in the chapters in greater depth. It is important that, in collaboration with teachers, professional development needs be carefully assessed so that the appropriate content can be selected to meet those needs.

Overview of Book Content

To begin each book in the series, Chapter 1 presents a literature review that defines the literacy component to be addressed in that book, explains why this component is important in the context of a complete and balanced literacy program, and synthesizes key research findings that underlie the recommendations for evidence-based instructional practices that follow in subsequent chapters. The conclusion of Chapter 1 invites professional development program participants to analyze, clarify, extend, and discuss the material presented in this chapter.

Chapter 2 outlines general principles for instruction. Participants are asked to evaluate their own instructional practices and to plan for refinement of those practices based on their students' needs. Each suggested instructional strategy in this chapter is based on the research presented in Chapter 1 and includes the purpose, necessary materials, and procedures for implementation. Ideas for engaging professional development participants in extended discussions related to phonemic awareness, phonics, vocabulary, fluency, or comprehension are offered at the end of Chapter 2.

Chapter 3 begins by presenting broad themes for effective assessment such as focusing on critical information, looking for patterns of behavior, recognizing developmental progressions, deciding how much assessment information is needed, using instructional situations for assessment purposes, using assessment information to guide instruction, and sharing assessment information with children and families. At the end of Chapter 3, professional development participants are asked to evaluate their current assessment practices, draw conclusions about needed change, and develop plans for change.

Chapter 4 addresses phonics instruction for English language learners (ELLs) and moves beyond classroom-based strategies by examining activities that can be recommended to families to support children's development of phonemic awareness, phonics, vocabulary, fluency, and comprehension at home. The final chapter provides a variety of print- and Web-based resources to support instruction in phonemic awareness, phonics, vocabulary, fluency, or comprehension.

Together, the information and activities included in these books, whether used as is or selectively, will foster careful consideration of research-based practice. Professional development participants will learn about the research that supports their current practices and will be guided to identify areas for improvement in their classroom programs.

The authors would like to thank the following reviewers for their valuable feedback: Lisa Joy DeMaagd, Taft Elementary School, Wyoming, MI, and Vickie McCullah-Jirash, Howe Elementary School, Howe, OK.

The need for new programs and methods for teaching reading is questionable. What is without question is the need for great teachers of reading—teachers who are effective, inspiring, and knowledgeable about children and reading. This series of books is our attempt to guide teachers into a deeper understanding of their craft and art—to help already good teachers become the great teachers that we need.

Introduction

Phonics

*T*hink back to your own early literacy school experiences. Do you remember being taught phonics? What kinds of instructional activities do you recall? What kinds of materials did your teachers use? Did you know why you were learning about sound–symbol relationships? Did your teachers help you understand that the whole point of phonics instruction is to provide strategies for dealing with unknown words? How was your phonics knowledge assessed?

Now think about the issues listed below. These may help you pinpoint areas that represent challenges in your current teaching situation. They may also help you focus on the most critical phonics instruction issues from your own perspective. Take some time now to write notes about your literacy program in general and your approach to phonics instruction in particular. We encourage you to discuss your responses with colleagues.

Book Club

What are the goals of your reading program?

_____

_____

_____

What are the goals of your phonics program?

_____

_____

_____

What is your daily schedule for teaching phonics? Is this schedule effective?

_____

_____

_____

Describe the materials you use for phonics instruction. Are they effective?

_____

_____

_____

How are parents involved in your phonics instruction?

_____

_____

_____

How do you assess students' phonics knowledge?

_____

_____

_____

Throughout this book, you will find places like these where we pause to ask you to reflect, write, and share. Our purpose is to encourage you to frame your interpretation and application of material in the book. We hope you will make notes about various aspects of planning and implementing effective phonics instruction. Record insights and ideas that are particularly pertinent to your own teaching situation. Doing so should provide you with "raw material" you can use to develop a plan for refining or altering your phonics instruction to provide more effective opportunities for your students to learn.

Phonics Instruction: What Does Research Tell Us?

2

....

CHAPTER 1

*Phonics
Instruction: What
Does Research
Tell Us?*

*Children learn much more than we teach them; they
often astound us with the creativity of their insights.
One goal of our teaching is to help children become
active examiners and analyzers of print. We want them
always to be searching for connections and patterns, to
form categories of knowledge, and to have a store of
examples to which they can refer.*

(PINNELL & FOUNTAS, 2003, P. 2)

*Probably no other aspect of reading instruction is more
discussed, more hotly debated, and less understood than
phonics and its role in learning to read.*

(STRICKLAND, 1998, P. 4)

*T*he role of phonics in learning to read has been a con-
tentious issue in both education and politics for well over
50 years! Clearly, few topics in the field of education have
engendered more emotional responses. Two leading schools of
thought, the phonics and whole-language approaches, polarized educators in the so-called "reading wars." Thankfully, this long-running
debate has evolved due to recent scientific understandings of how
children acquire literacy. These new understandings have led educators to pose more thoughtful questions. Today, virtually all educators agree that phonics holds an important place in children's literacy
development. Therefore, the question is no longer whether phonics
knowledge and skills should be taught, but how best to teach them.
The focus of the debate has shifted dramatically from arguing about
which method is better, to determining the appropriate combination
of each in a comprehensive reading program.

What Is Phonics?

In general terms, *phonics* refers to an understanding of the relationship
between letters and sounds as they are used in reading and writing.
This understanding includes knowledge of the alphabetic principle
or of the relationship between spoken sounds and letters or combi-
nations of letters. Consider the word *fish*. The first letter /f/ and the
pairing of the /sh/ at the end of the word each stand for a single, dis-
tinct sound.

Phonics and Phonemic Awareness: Are They the Same?

The terms *phonics* and *phonemic awareness* are frequently confused. Phonemic awareness is the understanding that a word is made up of sounds and the ability to manipulate sounds in spoken words (Adams, 1990; Beck & Juel, 1995). Phonics, on the other hand, refers to the relationship between speech and print. An easy way to remember the difference is that phonemic awareness does not involve any letters or print. It only involves working with the individual sound units (phonemes) in speech. When the goal of instruction shifts from speech to the speech–print connection, the instruction becomes phonics.

To illustrate, consider the following scenario. A kindergarten teacher and her class have been reciting the nursery rhyme "Little Miss Muffet" together. The teacher asks the children to say the rhyme again, but to clap every time they *hear* the /m/ sound at the beginning of the word. The children are happy to "put on their listening ears" as they excitedly clap when they hear the /m/ sound at the beginning of the words *Miss* and *Muffet*. Afterward, the teacher displays a chart where the "Little Miss Muffet" rhyme has been written. This time the teacher asks the children to clap when they *see* the letter that stands for the /m/ sound. Finally, the teacher sends the children back to their tables with individual copies of the nursery rhyme and highlighters. The children practice reading the poem and highlight words that begin with /m/.

Keeping in mind that phonemic awareness does not involve letters or print, we can easily see that the phonemic awareness segment of the lesson ends and the phonics portion of the lesson begins when the teacher displays the poem on chart paper.

Why Is Phonics Important?

Knowledge of phonics is necessary for successful independent reading.

ROUTMAN & BUTLER, 1995, P. 2

Not too long ago, there was a popular bumper sticker that read, "So many books, so little time!" We suspect that maxim is one with which many educators would heartily agree. Teachers tend to lead very print-rich lives. On your desk or nightstand, you may have quite a variety

4
....
CHAPTER 1
*Phonics
Instruction: What
Does Research
Tell Us?*

of reading materials ranging from professional texts and journals to novels and magazines, and perhaps even "how to" manuals and cookbooks! In fact, if you were to examine the text in closest proximity to you right now, you would probably be able to recognize all of the words *and* understand the meaning. This is exactly what is expected of any mature reader. Now, consider the novice reader who faces a far more difficult task. Less experienced readers must grapple with many unfamiliar words and still be able to extract the meaning of a given text. Yet, encountering too many new words will most certainly impede comprehension. How can we support young readers in resolving word identification issues so that they may fully comprehend and learn from written text? Clearly, helping children to acquire phonics knowledge is an essential ingredient in becoming a more capable reader.

Phonics has been the focus of countless research studies. The bulk of this research has centered on the usefulness of phonics instruction and the most appropriate methods to teach children about sound–symbol relationships. The following findings, based on this research, provide a rationale for including high-quality phonics instruction in any effective early reading program.

1. Virtually all children can benefit from phonics instruction. "We cannot afford not to teach phonics" (Fox, 2004, p. iii).

Regardless of the program or the kind of instruction received, all children learn about letter–sound correspondences, spelling patterns, and pronunciations as part of the process of becoming literate. Children need to understand these relationships in order to read and write. Children also need ample opportunities to practice and review these new understandings. Phonics instruction is the medium for children to explore, internalize, and apply this new knowledge so that they can gradually achieve greater facility and independence with reading and writing. It stands to reason, then, that virtually all children can profit from quality phonics instruction that is purposefully and meaningfully embedded into the early reading program.

2. Phonics knowledge positively affects decoding ability. "Let's start with the purpose of teaching phonics, which is to be able to decode words. Given this purpose, it follows that very early in the instructional sequence children should experience decoding some words" (Beck, 2006, p. 27).

To become proficient readers, students must be able to rapidly and correctly identify words. They must become skilled at decoding words. Decoding words involves converting the printed word into spoken language. It requires the student to retrieve the sounds for a given word. For example, if the child sees the letters *f*, *a*, and *n*, the word *fan* may be recognized instantly. If the reader is confronted by a word such as *transmogrification*, there may be a slight delay in articulation of the word. When readers identify words without hesitation, this immediate response is known as *automaticity*. However, when a word is identified after deliberation, this process is called *decoding* or *word attack*.

Phonics knowledge positively influences the ability to decode (Stanovich & West, 1989). This makes early acquisition of decoding skills desirable because this ability is a powerful predictor of future skill in reading comprehension (Beck & Juel, 1995; Lundberg, 1984). The notion that successful readers learn decoding early is well documented in studies of literacy development (Chall, 1983; Cunningham & Stanovich, 1997; Ehri, 1994; Moats, 1998). As Beck (2006, p. 12) insists, "I learned that children must gain control of the print-to-speech mapping system *early* if they are to become successful readers." The National Reading Panel (2000) recommends that phonics be taught in the early grades, and Armbruster and Osborn (2001) specify that phonics instruction is most effective when it begins in kindergarten or first grade. As a general guideline, two years of phonics instruction should be sufficient for the majority of children. So, those receiving phonics instruction beginning in kindergarten should be completed with it by the end of first grade. Likewise, children beginning phonics instruction in first grade should finish the program by the end of second grade. However, word study continues throughout children's lives.

3. Phonics knowledge promotes understanding of the alphabetic principle.

The primary objective of all reading instruction is for each child to become an independent, enthusiastic reader and writer empowered to think critically about text. Toward this end, it is essential that the child be able to recognize frequently encountered words accurately and instantly. In order for this automatic word recognition to occur, children need a basic understanding of their language. For readers of English, an alphabetic language system, children must have a strong grasp of the *alphabetic principle*, which involves acquiring an appreciation of the speech–print connection—that there are systematic relationships between letters and sounds.

6
....

CHAPTER 1

*Phonics
Instruction: What
Does Research
Tell Us?*

Two powerful indicators of reading success that are requisite to understanding the alphabetic principle are *alphabet recognition* (knowing the letter names and sounds) and *phonemic awareness* (awareness of speech sounds) (Adams, 1990). Blevins (2006, p. 20) describes alphabet recognition and phonemic awareness as "the two skills [that] open the gate for early reading." He goes on to say that in the absence of these, children cannot learn to read. In other words, children who do not master the alphabetic principle in the early grades are likely to continue to fall further behind their classmates as children are expected to do greater amounts of independent reading (Stanovich, 1986).

However, with a strong foundation in letter knowledge and phonemic awareness, an understanding of alphabetic principle is well within the reach of the young reader-to-be. Once the principle is discovered, the child is well equipped to decipher unfamiliar words in print. In addition, he or she can construct readable, although not always correct, spellings that will become increasingly precise as more experience with reading and writing is acquired.

4. Phonics knowledge improves spelling ability. "**It must always be kept in mind, however, that phonics does not stand alone. It is used during reading and spelling and its use is informed by reading and spelling. In other words, readers use what they learn about phonics during writing, and writers are helped to spell by what they have learned about phonics through reading**" **(Strickland, 1998, p. 25).**

In many ways, reading and writing are reciprocal processes. Readers use phonics to decode, blending sounds together to identify and pronounce printed words. Conversely, spelling involves encoding, taking spoken words apart in order to isolate sounds to construct written words. Writers apply phonics as they spell the words needed to express thoughts and to communicate with others.

Experts agree that becoming a speller is a cognitively complex process. Knowledge of spelling, or the *orthographic system*, begins to unfold long before a child enters school. The classic research of Charles Read (1971, 1975) was instrumental in creating an awareness among educators that preschoolers' spelling inventions possess a phonetic logic and develop in predictable ways over time (Rasinski & Padak, 2001).

Read's work gave rise to a line of developmental spelling inquiry led by Edmund Henderson, often referred to as the Virginia Studies. This cornerstone research confirmed that there is indeed a systematic nature to children's developmental or invented spellings, which extends far beyond the preschool years. Moreover, children's invented spellings share a common developmental sequence that signifies their level of understanding about how words work. Understanding that children's misspellings contain critical diagnostic information helps teachers to provide more differentiated instruction not only in the area of phonics and spelling but also in vocabulary.

Henderson (1990) advised teachers to use spelling assessment results in order to select appropriate instructional strategies when teaching alphabet study, word recognition, phonics, vocabulary, and spelling (Bear, Invernizzi, Templeton, & Johnston, 2007). The model of instruction that combines all of these areas is known as *word study* (Henderson, 1990; Henderson & Beers, 1980). Bear and colleagues (2007) describe the purpose of word study as "to examine words in order to reveal consistencies within our written language system and to help students master the recognition, spelling, and meaning of specific words" (p. 5).

Frequent opportunities for children to write and spell are essential ingredients of an effective, comprehensive literacy program. Young children's attempts at spelling unfamiliar words involve their thinking about the sounds that they hear. This temporary or invented spelling draws on the same underlying word knowledge as the process of reading words. Thus, encouraging children to write and, more important, to try to write what they want to say, is a great way to support students' phonics and word recognition development. Opportunities to write and spell should be part of word-learning programs. A detailed examination of the ways in which children develop as spellers is beyond the scope of this book. Several key resources are listed in Chapter 5, however, for those interested in pursuing this important topic.

5. Phonics knowledge leads to increased fluency and comprehension. "The purpose of phonics instruction is not that children learn to sound out words. The purpose is that they learn to recognize words, quickly and automatically, so they can turn their attention to comprehension of the text" (Stahl, 1992, p. 66).

The goal of phonics instruction goes well beyond teaching children to "sound it out." Rasinski and Padak (2001) emphasize that the goal for teachers should not be readers skilled at decoding and word recognition regardless of whether or not meaning is constructed from the text. Instead, educators should aim to develop "fluent readers who read efficiently, expressively, and meaningfully so that meaning can be easily be constructed by the reader" (p. xv). In other words, teach children to use phonics so that they can read!

8
....

CHAPTER 1

*Phonics
Instruction: What
Does Research
Tell Us?*

Nonfluent readers read slowly, often with hesitations and inaccuracies, and devote so much mental energy to decoding and word solving that comprehension is interrupted and diminished. Thus, fluent reading is a major objective of reading instruction because decoding print effortlessly empowers readers to devote more of their conscious attention or mental energy to understanding text during reading. So, it is apparent that phonics knowledge is critically linked to both fluency and comprehension. Chard, Pikulski, and McDonagh (2006) describe the relationship among phonics, fluency, and comprehension this way: "Fluency is part of a developmental process of building oral language and decoding skills that form a bridge to comprehension, resulting in a reciprocal causal relationship with reading comprehension" (p. 40). In fact, the hallmark of fluent reading is the ability to decode and comprehend at the same time (Blevins, 2006; Samuels, 2006).

The Issue of Scope and Sequence

In much of the literature, teachers are implored to teach phonics *systematically*. Systematic instruction unfolds from basic to more complex. This presents a challenge for teachers who may wonder about the appropriate sequence for instruction in sound–spelling relationships. We have adapted the following suggestions about sequence of teaching phonics and related skills from Blevins (2006):

- **Teach short-vowel sounds before long-vowel sounds.**
- **Teach consonants and short vowels in combination.** This enables children to read words rather quickly, which will provide them with plenty of natural and authentic practice. "Phonics is useless if it can't be applied, and what is not applied is not learned" (Blevins, 2006, p. 115). Throughout this book, you will find multiple examples of activities that draw children's attention to onsets (initial sounds) and rimes (word families) that serve this important purpose.
- **Be sure that the majority of the consonants taught early on are continuous consonants such as** *f, l, m, n,* **and** *s.* Try saying one of these sounds and then a consonant like *b, d,* or *g,* and you'll see how much easier the former are for teaching blending.
- **Teach higher-frequency letters and letter patterns first.** This enables children to decode many words early on, which is a strong motivator.

- **Progress from simple to more complex sound-spellings.** For example, teach simple consonant sounds before digraphs (*sh, ch, th, wh, ph, gh, ng*) and blends (*br, cl, st,* etc.). Here is a suggested sequence:

Short vowels and consonants in combination
Digraphs (*ch, sh, th, wh*)
Blends (*r*-blends, *s*-blends, *l*-blends)
Final *e* (*a_e, e_e, i_e, o_e, u_e*)
Long vowels (multiple spellings)
Variant vowels (*oo, au, aw*) **and diphthongs** (*ou, ow, oi, oy*)
Silent letters, inflectional endings (*-ed, -s, -ing*)

Teachers also need to make decisions regarding the scope of the phonics instruction. *Scope* refers to the identification of the most high-utility sound-spelling relationships. Those used most frequently need to be taught directly and explicitly since students will encounter them repeatedly in the process of reading and writing. Infrequent sound-spelling relationships can be learned at the point of need (or perhaps ignored all together). Again, we have adapted Blevins's (2006) suggestions regarding scope:

- **Kindergarten:**
  Blending (use CVC pattern)
- **First Grade:**
  Blending and word building
  Short vowels
  Long vowel digraphs (*ai, ay, ea, ee, oa, ow,* etc.)
  Consonant clusters or blends (*br, cl, st,* etc.)
  Consonant digraphs (*ch, sh, th, wh,* etc.)
- **Grades 2–3:**
  More complex vowel spellings
  Multisyllabic words

Components of Successful Phonics Programs

Active. Social. Reflective. These three words best express the phonics instruction to strive for in your classroom. Look to design a program that makes children aware of what they're doing, why they're doing it, and how they are progressing . . . never lose sight of your goal to give

*children a basic understanding of the alphabetic princi-
ple and to use this insight to read for pleasure and
information.*

(*Blevins, 2006, p. 113*)

Up to this point in the chapter, we have defined phonics and have outlined why phonics is important in the reading programs of young children. A suggested scope and sequence has been offered to assist you in
developing a phonics program that provides systematic and in-depth
attention to decoding instruction in the context of beginning reading
and writing activities. We conclude this discussion by providing some
key tenets of successful phonics programs. Based on extensive research
in the area of phonics (Blevins, 2006; Dahl, Scharer, Lawson, & Groa-
gan, 2001; Routman, 2003; Stahl, 1992; Tompkins, 2003), the following eight research-based reminders are offered as guidelines for
successful phonics instruction in your classroom.

1. Teachers understand that phonics knowledge is developmental.
   Children proceed developmentally through the stages of writing
   because children gain much phonics knowledge through
   spelling attempts in their writing.

2. Phonics instruction builds on a foundation of phonemic awareness and knowledge of how language works.

3. Teachers use a combination of phonics approaches: (a) systematic, direct, explicit instruction and (b) phonics learned in
   context, at the point of need and use. These are the "teachable
   moments" when teachers can incorporate phonics information
   informally into real reading and writing activities.

4. Formal phonics instruction draws to a close by the end of second grade. Beyond second grade, children continue developing
   word knowledge through spelling, writing, and word study.

5. The emphasis is on reading words in connected text rather than
   rule memorization. Teachers provide repeated opportunities for
   students to apply learned sound-spelling relationships to reading and writing. Reading and phonics are not taught as separate
   entities. Effective phonics instruction teaches children the most
   frequently used letter–sound patterns. Children's growing
   understandings of how words work are further refined and
   enhanced through plenty of opportunities to read.

6. Teachers teach high-utility phonics (the phonics concepts, skills,
   and generalizations that are most useful for decoding and

spelling unfamiliar words). Instruction includes blending and attention to onsets and rimes.

7. Word-recognition strategies are developed as the internal structure of words is taught.

8. Automaticity and fluency are developed so that students' mental energies are available for the important work of comprehending text.

Conclusion

A firm working knowledge of letter–sound relationships is absolutely essential for successful reading to occur (Fox, 2003; NRP, 2000). However, phonics instruction cannot be a total reading program. Proficient decoders are meaning-focused word solvers. That is, they double-check to make sure that words sounded out make sense in the context in which they appear. Programs that place an inordinate emphasis on the teaching of letter–sound relationships and not enough on their application in meaningful reading and writing are of questionable value. In providing effective phonics instruction, teachers need to begin with the end in mind so that students understand that the goal of learning letter sounds is to transfer this knowledge to daily reading and writing activities. In the next chapter, research-based suggestions for teaching phonics and specific instructional strategies will be presented.

Professional Development Suggestions

ACED: Analysis, Clarification, Extension, Discussion

I. REFLECTION (10 TO 15 MINUTES)

ANALYSIS:

- What, for you, were the most interesting and/or important ideas in this chapter?

  _____
  _____
  _____

- What information was new to you?

  _____
  _____

CLARIFICATION:

- Did anything surprise you? Confuse you?

  _____
  _____

EXTENSION:

- What questions do you have?

  _____
  _____
  _____

II. DISCUSSION (20 MINUTES)

- Form groups of 4 to 6 members
- Appoint a *facilitator (timer)* and *recorder*.
- Share responses. Make sure that each person has shared his or her responses to each category (Analysis/ Clarification/ Extension).
- Help each other with any areas of confusion.
- Answer and/or discuss questions raised by group members.

- On chart paper, the recorder should summarize main discussion points and identify issues or questions the group would like to raise for general discussion.

III. APPLICATION (10 MINUTES)

- Based on your reflection and discussion, how might you apply what you have learned from this literature review about the teaching of phonics?

_____

_____

_____

_____

_____

CHAPTER 2

Instructional Strategies for Phonics Development

Several years ago, near the end of August, Belinda received a phone call from a former graduate student, Kristen, who excitedly said that she had just landed a job as a first-grade teacher in a rural school district. It was obvious she was ecstatic. After plenty of well-wishes and congratulatory remarks were shared, Kristen said that she needed advice on the effective teaching of phonics.

Kristen was concerned by a conversation she had with the principal who had hired her. The principal explained that in his school, all primary teachers were required to teach 30 minutes of systematic, explicit phonics instruction each day. The principal then handed her the required phonics workbook. Kristen practically gasped aloud when she saw it because it was the same plaid-covered phonics book she had used as a first-grader! The principal gave her an empathetic look and said that the current board of education adopted this phonics program in response to the district's falling test scores in reading. Apparently, they believed that this type of phonics instruction was the mainstay of an effective reading program and that using this text was non-negotiable since it was a board-approved text. Perhaps observing the look of dismay on Kristen's face, the principal told Kristen that he encouraged the teachers to use the program flexibly, although he had to admit that most of the teachers were using the program as prescribed in the manual. The principal then presented Kristen with the keys to her classroom and reminded her that his door would always be open to her for support and guidance.

After Kristen shared her story, Belinda jokingly responded, "Welcome to the real world of teaching!" Kristen did not seem to find the humor in that remark. So, all joking was put aside, and they set out to address the dilemma of how to implement the phonics program flexibly. They knew that "flexible use" would include research-based/best practice strategies for teaching phonics to Kristen's first-graders. So, they began to review the strategies of best practices recommended by the experts in the teaching of phonics.

Belinda suggested that Kristen begin her search by reviewing the literature on why phonics is important and the principles of effective phonics instruction. Chapter 1 of this book highlights these topics and also offers a scope and sequence related to the issue of "systematic instruction." From there, the search for the most effective strategies was underway. Kristen's situation propelled us to select and compile research-based strategies for teaching phonics. The strategies are outlined in the following section to make them readily accessible for teachers like Kristen, and for all of us in the business of providing exemplary phonics instruction for primary-aged children.

Professional Development Suggestions

Before adding new strategies and activities to your instructional repertoire, it is important to evaluate your current teaching practices: What current phonics instructional practices do you find to be effective? What areas need to be fine-tuned? Are there instructional components that are not being covered to the extent that they need to be?

To help you in evaluating your current practices, consider the semantic feature analysis chart on the next page. Along the side of the chart, you will see space for you to list those instructional strategies that you currently use to enhance children's phonics knowledge. Across the top of the chart, you will see components that may be present in the activities that you listed. Of course, not every component can, or should, be part of every activity. Collectively, however, the activities should provide balance so that a range of developmental levels and diverse learner needs can be effectively addressed.

Take the time to complete the semantic feature analysis chart. Place a + sign in the corresponding box for each attribute that is present in a phonics instructional activity that you currently use. More than one attribute may be present for each activity that you list. You may wish to collaborate with colleagues, as doing so may help you recall the additional strategies you use over the course of a school year.

When the semantic feature analysis is complete, it should help you see which aspects of phonics instruction currently receive a great deal of attention in your classroom and which may not receive enough emphasis. Knowing this will help you to better plan adjustments in your instructional routine. Discuss your findings and insights with colleagues.

Strategy Suggestions

The phonics strategies described in this section have all been found effective through research. In general, each can be adapted to work successfully with children in grades K through 3. In the descriptions, we list common procedures and materials, but we encourage you to innovate to meet the needs of your students!

Semantic Feature Analysis Chart

Phonics Strategies	Develop-mentally Appropriate	Builds on Phonemic Awareness	Systematic Instruction	Phonics in Context	High-Utility Information	Onsets and Rimes	Writing and Spelling

Action Phonics

Purpose:

To teach children beginning sound–letter relationships.

Materials:

Action Phonics Cards (large cards with a capital and lowercase letters on one side and the "action word" on the reverse side of the card)

Description:

- Action Phonics teaches the beginning letter- and letter combination-sound associations through physical actions or movements that begin with the targeted sound. The actions for Action Phonics (adapted from Cunningham, 1987) are listed in Figure 2.1.

Figure 2.1

Actions for Action Phonics

b	bounce	**t**	talk	**fl**	fly
c	catch	**v**	vacuum	**fr**	frown
d	dance	**w**	walk, wiggle	**gl**	glare, glue
f	fall	**y**	yawn, yell	**gr**	grab
g	gallop	**z**	zip	**pl**	plant
h	hop, hum	**ch**	cheer	**pr**	print
j	jump	**sh**	shiver, shout	**sw**	swallow
k	kick	**th**	think	**sk**	skate, skip
l	lick	**wh**	whistle	**sl**	sleep
m	march	**br**	breathe	**sm**	smile
n	nod	**bl**	blow, blink	**sp**	spin
p	paint, pat	**cr**	crawl, cry	**st**	stand still, stop
q	quiet	**cl**	climb	**tr**	trip
r	run, rip	**dr**	drive	**tw**	twist
s	sit				

Source: Rasinski and Padak (2001, p. 48). Reprinted with permission.

20
....

CHAPTER 2

*Instructional
Strategies for
Phonics
Development*

- Beginning and struggling readers often have difficulty committing letters and sounds to their permanent memories. Teaching these sounds through Action Phonics requires students to move their bodies, which serves to buttress students' memories of the letters and sounds. Rasinski and Padak (2001, p. 47) liken the physical movement to a "conceptual glue that holds the sound and symbol together until they are thoroughly learned."

- After students have learned the Action Phonics letters and their associated movements, teachers can expect to frequently observe the children making the actions at their seats as they try to read or spell words on their own.

- **Teaching Tip**: Two key letters and sounds to teach early on are *s* (*s*it) and *q* (*q*uiet). These two letters are a natural way to bring this action-packed activity to an end!

Procedures:

1. Select the Action Phonics cards to be taught (usually 1 or 2 per week for kindergartners and 2 through 4 for first-graders).

2. Begin an Action Phonics lesson by conducting a quick review of all the previously learned consonants, actions, and sounds.

3. Then introduce the new initial consonant with its accompanying movement and sound.

4. When you raise the card overhead, the children perform the designated action. When you lower the card, this is the signal for the children to stop or "freeze." Raise and lower the same card several times before moving on to the next card, giving the children multiple opportunities to practice.

5. Before moving on to the next card, it is helpful to periodically remind the children how Action Phonics can help readers solve unknown words. Your explicit language can empower children to begin to employ this first-letter decoding strategy as a means of independently solving unknown words. So, for example, you might say:

"Let's say when you are reading later on today, you come to a tricky word that begins with this letter [teacher points to the Action Phonics card at hand]. Since you know Action Phonics, you may be able to figure out the word all by yourself. When we do not know a word, sometimes it helps if we can get our mouths ready for the beginning sound. To help you to get your mouth ready for the beginning sound, you can think about our Action Phonics cards. Thinking of the action that goes along with the letter will help you to get your mouth ready for the first sound. Let's practice getting our mouths ready for this one right now."

Target Letter Transport (also called Spotlight Letter Strategy)

Purpose (adapted from Beck, 2006, pp. 31–38):

To assist children in learning targeted letter–sound relationships in all positions in which they are found in words.

Materials:

- Large letter cards to use for demonstration.
- Pocket chart for displaying the large letter cards.
- A set of individual letter cards for each student.
- Individual Word Pockets for each student to use in sorting and displaying letters. These can be made of oak tag that is fastened on the ends with glue and folded to create a pocket.

Description:

- Once students learn to decode the first letter in the word, they have to be able to recognize that same targeted or spotlighted letter and its corresponding sound in all positions in which it is found in words. Research shows that some students, especially those who struggle, often have considerable difficulty decoding both medial and final graphemes in words (Beck, 2006; McCandliss, Beck, Sandak, & Perfetti, 2003).

- There is some evidence that teaching letter–sound correspondences may be more effective when phonemic awareness and phonics instruction are combined (Beck, 2006; National Reading Panel, 2000). In the Target Letter Transport activity, phonemic awareness instruction is intentionally integrated into the teaching of letter–sound associations to enhance the effectiveness of phonics instruction.

Procedures:

1. Utilize children's phonemic awareness abilities by drawing their attention to the sound represented by a targeted letter in the initial position.
2. Link the printed letter with its corresponding sound.
3. Explicitly distinguish among words that have the targeted letter sound in the initial position and those that do not.

4. Activate and build phonemic awareness by directing children's attention to the sound represented by the targeted letter in the final position.

5. Distinguish words that have the targeted letter sound in the final position from those that do not.

6. Compare words that have the targeted letter sound in the initial and final positions.

The following sample lesson, adapted from Beck (2006) shows how these six steps come to life in the context of classroom learning.

Sample Lesson for Teaching the Letter-Sound Correspondence for /s/

Lesson Focus	Procedure	Please Note . . .
1. Create awareness of target sound in the initial position.	T: My dog Sammy is very silly. He likes to play tug-of-war with old socks. What does Sammy like to play with? The words Sammy, silly, and sock begin with the same sound: the /s/ sound. Watch my mouth: /s/. (You say /s/.)	This procedure activates phonemic awareness by focusing attention on the target sound.
2. Connect the printed letter with the sound the letter represents.	Show children the large letter s card. T: This is the letter s. The letter s stands for the /s/ sound in Sammy, silly, and sock. You say /s/. Each time I touch the letter s, say /s/ (Touch s several times).	The point of the whole lesson is to connect a printed letter with its sound, which happens in this step. However, this doesn't provide enough practice to solidify the learning. Thus, it is important to proceed to the next step.
3. Discriminate among words that start with /s/ and those that do not.	Students will now need their own letter s cards. T: If the word I say begins with the /s/ sound, hold up your s card and say /s/. If it doesn't begin with the /s/ sound, shake your head no. (Examples: Sally, salt, sea, monkey, many, house),	This step provides additional practice in identifying the /s/ phoneme at the beginning of words and saying the sound in the presence of the letter s.

Lesson Focus	Procedure	Please Note . . .
4. Develop phonemic awareness of target sound in the final position.	T: A football player who throws the ball makes a _____. [pass] Explain that pass ends with the letter s, the letter that stands for the /s/ sound. Say some more words that end with the letter s, and have students repeat them. (Examples: toss, brass, glass)	This step, which moves the targeted letter to the final position, helps children learn that a given letter often represents the same sound in other positions in words.
5. Distinguish words that end in /s/ from words that do not.	This step is similar to step 3 except that the focus is on the final position. T: I'll say some words. If the word ends with the /s/ sound, hold up your s card. If it doesn't end with the /s/ sound, put your s card behind your back. (Examples: drinks, hams, treats, broom, dream, drink)	In this step students identify /s/ at the end of words and say /s/ in the presence of the letter s.
6. Compare words that have /s/ in the initial and final positions.	Students will need their Word Pockets. T: If the word begins with /s/, put your letter s at the beginning of the Word Pocket. If the word ends with /s/, put your letter s at the end of the Word Pocket. (Examples: salt, grass, swim, mouse)	In addition to providing practice, the requirement that they place their letters at the beginning or end of their Word Pockets connects the phonemic position with the visual position.

Next Steps:

- Beck (2006) advocates using the preceding six-step process to teach consonant digraphs (ch, sh, th, wh). The letters of the digraph should appear on one card and children should simply be told that the letters /ch/, for example, stand for the /ch/ sound in words like chin and chair.

- The six steps may also be used for introducing short vowels, except that the teaching sequence goes from initial position to the medial position. Beck advises devoting more time to the vowel in the medial position since medial vowels are often quite challenging for beginning and struggling readers.

Teaching Onsets and Rimes

Purpose:

After initial letters and sounds are introduced, students' attention can be directed to how to construct the remainder of the word. Teaching children that many words contain easily identifiable "chunks" (also known as *word families, rimes,* and *phonograms*) allows children to make an important discovery. When young readers can search for and locate these chunks on their own, they are on their way toward becoming proficient decoders.

Description:

- *Onsets* are the consonants that precede the vowels in words and syllables (Examples: the *s* in the word *sap;* the *sl* in the word *slap* or the *str* in the word *strap*). Once students have some of these onsets under control, you can begin rime instruction. A *rime* is the combination of a vowel and the consonants that follow it in a syllable (Examples: *op* in the word *mop; ick* in the word *stick; eet* in the word *street*). Rimes are also referred to as *phonograms, word families,* and *word chunks.*

- Some experts advocate that vowel sounds be taught, not in isolation, but in the context of the consonants that follow them in syllables. Other experts add that onset/rime instruction is more effective than having students memorize vowel generalizations and rules. Clymer's (1963) classic study of the utility of teaching phonics rules/generalizations showed that many of 45 rule generalizations have limited usefulness. For example, he found that the most well-known rule, "When two vowels go a-walking the first one does the talking," is only accurate about 45 percent of the time. In other words, this rule has more exceptions than not. Teaching children a rule with this many exceptions is obviously of questionable value.

- Rimes, on the other hand, are a productive approach to phonics instruction (Rasinski & Padak, 2001). Since rimes consist of several letters, decoding by rime enables the reader to dissect a word several letters at a time, or in "chunks." This is often easier than analyzing individual letters one at a time. In addition, rimes are reliable and generalizable (Blevins, 2006), which makes them an appealing approach for teaching vowel sounds and for word-solving as well. Rasinski and Padak (2001, p. 49) elaborate on this point:

Rimes have a high degree of consistency. When the rime -*ack* appears in a word, it nearly always makes *ak*; and when -*it* appears at the end of a syllable, it almost invariably makes *it*. In addition, by their very nature, words containing the same rime, do rhyme. Thus, it is not difficult to compose poems that feature targeted rimes for children, providing superb practice in learning those rimes. Moreover, it is easy for students to write and celebrate their own rhyming poetry as they begin to understand the connection between the written rimes and their corresponding sounds.

- Another benefit of onset/rime instruction is that a great number of words can be generated from a relatively short list of phonograms. This is highly beneficial, since it would be quite time consuming to teach children all of the estimated 353 rimes that can be used to produce at least two common one-syllable words (Fry, 1998)! Thus, it makes sense to teach those rimes with the greatest utility, those that can be used to decode the greatest number of words. Edward Fry (1998) has identified 38 rimes that can be used to make 654 one-syllable words (see Figure 2.2) and decode several thousand multisyllabic words. Depending on the age and grade level of the student, the entire list of 38 rimes may be covered during the course of a school year.

- So, now that we have established the importance and advantages of incorporating onset/rime instruction into the teaching of phonics, the question becomes how to most effectively carry out this instruction in the classroom. On the next few pages, you will find a variety of strategies for encouraging students to apply knowledge of onsets and rimes to decoding, word recognition, and spelling.

Teaching Tip:

We suggest you use the list shown in Figure 2.2 as a resource for determining which rimes to teach. Some teachers find it helpful to group rimes into logical sets, such as those with the same short vowel sounds (e.g., *at, am, ag, ack, ank, ap, an*) and the same long vowel sounds (e.g., *ay, ail, ain, ake*) (Rasinski & Zimmerman, 2001). Many teachers report that they work through all of the short vowel rime patterns first, one vowel sound at a time, and then this process is repeated with the long vowel rime patterns. As students develop greater proficiency with rimes, you may want to have children compare and contrast them. First, the rimes may be compared by the ending consonants of the same short vowel sound (e.g., -*at*, -*ack*). Next,

Figure 2.2

The Most Common Rimes

1. –ay	20. –ug
2. –ill	21. –op
3. –ip	22. –in
4. –at	23. –an
5. –am	24. –est
6. –ag	25. –ink
7. –ack	26. –ow
8. –ank	27. –ew
9. –ick	28. –ore
10. –ell	29. –ed
11. –ot	30. –ab
12. –ing	31. –ob
13. –ap	32. –ock
14. –unk	33. –ake
15. –ail	34. –ine
16. –ain	35. –ight
17. –eed	36. –im
18. –y	37. –uck
19. –out	38. –um

Source: Fry (1998)

compare different short vowel rimes (e.g., *-at, -it*). Finally, compare and contrast rimes with the same written vowel symbol, but using those that represent long and short vowel sounds (e.g., *-at, -ate*) (Johnston, 1999; Rasinski & Zimmerman, 2001).

Three-Day Rime Time Routine

Purpose:

To teach children to decode through rime recognition.

Materials:

Chart paper, markers, student copies of word family poems (rime time poems).

Description:

- After the general sequence for teaching the rimes has been determined, you need a systematic routine for presenting the rimes to the students. Routines are helpful because they tend to maximize use of instructional time.

- Although no routine works for all teachers and children, the following three-day "rime time" approach has been successful for many children.

- This Three-Day Rime Time Routine teaches one rime per week and is often recommended for mid-to-end-of-year kindergartners and first-graders, depending on the progress and needs of the learners.

Procedures (adapted from Rasinski & Zimmerman, 2001):

Day 1

1. Before the lesson, select the rime time poem to be taught and copy it onto chart paper. The poem should contain the rime to be learned. The poem should be displayed. Gather the children together in an area where everyone can easily see the poem.

2. Read the poem to the children, modeling expressive fluent reading.

3. Then reread the poem. This time, point to each word in the poem as it is being read. Ask the children to chime in.

4. Now reread the poem chorally with *all* the children.

5. Ask if any of the children have spotted the rime time words in this poem. After just a week or two of participating in the Rime Time Routine, the children begin to search for the words "that have something alike about them" almost immediately!

6. Ask volunteers to come up to the chart paper and highlight the rime time words.

Day 2

1. Review the rime time poem by rereading it a few times. It is fun for the children when you select the next group of poem readers creatively. For example, you may want to begin by having the entire class reread the poem chorally. Next, only those who

28
....

CHAPTER 2

*Instructional
Strategies for
Phonics
Development*

have summer birthdays read the poem. Then you may ask that only those with Velcro on their shoes read the poem. You get the idea! The group not reading the poem aloud can clap (or touch their noses, or high five, or some other such action) whenever one of the rime time words is read. This helps to ensure that all of the students are actively involved in closely monitoring the text as they search for the targeted rimes.

2. You may want to extend the students' learning by drawing their attention to the individual words that contain particular elements, such as certain letters, blends, or digraphs. Attention may also be directed to punctuation, high-frequency words, and so forth, that are found in the poem.

3. Now list the rime time words on chart paper. Ask the children to help you add other words containing the rime. Display these chart papers around the room so that students may frequently review the words and incorporate them into their writing. Children can also record the words in their journals or personal spelling dictionaries. Composition notebooks work well for this because they are inexpensive and take up less space than standard spiral notebooks.

4. Distribute photocopies of the poem to the students. Ask students to read the poem in partners. First, the partners read the poem together. Then the students read the poem independently to one another, offering positive feedback, encouragement, and assistance to each other as needed. The partners finish by reading the poem one more time together.

5. Select a few of the poetry partners to perform the poem for the class. The class applauds after each performance.

6. Poems may be placed into students' poetry notebooks. You may want students to take their poetry notebooks home once a week to share poems with family members or friends. These "Lucky Listeners" sign the poetry notebook and may leave positive and encouraging comments about the child's developing progress as a reader.

Day 3

1. Through the repeated reading of the poems in Days 1 and 2 of the Rime Time Routine, students begin to develop a sense for how these poems are constructed. Thus, by Day 3, the students are ready to compose their own rime time poem. Of course, the

key to success here is for you to *model* this process over and over again before sending the children off to write their own poems. In fact, when working with kindergarten or beginning first-graders, the poem writing is best accomplished as a teacher-guided, whole- or small-group activity. However, beyond this, students will be able to begin to construct the poems in small groups, partners, and/or individually. The list of words on the chart from Day 2 can be of great assistance to the students in trying to create these rime time poems. Here is an example of a poem that a struggling first-grader wrote on his own in mid-March:

> *The leprechaun played a trick*
> *On a boy named Patrick.*
> *He said the gold was under the stick.*
> *When Patrick told Rick,*
> *The leprechaun ran away*
> *QUICK, QUICK, QUICK!*
> *By Alex Latturi**

2. Students transfer their poems to chart paper or blank overhead projector transparencies, or enter them into the computer. (It is not unusual for first-graders to be able to do poetry PowerPoint presentations these days!) Once this is completed, the poems on the chart paper may be displayed around the room or the ones on the overhead and computer may be used for the children to read and practice at centers.

3. Regardless of the media used, the students may now move about the classroom, reading and re-reading the poems that their classmates have written. It should be no surprise that in Belinda's first-grade classroom, these were often the most widely read texts in the room!

4. You and the students may also opt to move about the classroom in groups to carry out the poem reading. The author has the honor of reading the poem first. Then the poem is read chorally a couple of times and individually by volunteer students. Next, you and the student work together to "teach the poem," drawing the children's attention to the key words in the poem. Then the group moves on to the next poem.

*Reprinted by permission.

30
....

CHAPTER 2

*Instructional
Strategies for
Phonics
Development*

5. By the end of the Three-Day Rime Time Routine, most of the students will have mastered the targeted rime. In addition, students will have definitely developed a deeper appreciation for poetry and the work of poets, for they have been involved in the creation of poetry to share with others in an authentic format. These poems can later be collected, typed, copied, and bound in the form of a class-authored book for each student to read and celebrate his or her own authorship of published poetry (Rasinski & Zimmerman, 2001).

Five-Day Rime Time Routine

Purpose:

To teach children to decode through rime recognition.

Materials:

Chart paper, markers, student copies of word family poems (rime time poems).

Description:

- The following is a five-day sequence of activities for teaching *two* rimes per week. Two rimes per week is often recommended for mid-to-end-of-year first-graders and second-graders. Of course, this depends on the progress and needs of the learners.

- In addition, the five-day plan differs from the three-day plan in another important way. The three-day lesson proceeds from whole–part–whole, but the five-day plan proceeds from part–whole. Although it is important to frequently contextualize instruction from whole–part–whole, especially when the students are first learning how to decode through rime instruction, the "parts" matter too. In his book, *Breaking the Code: The New Science of Beginning Reading and Writing*, Gentry (2006, p. 41) addresses this issue:

  > Both the whole and parts are important (Strickland, 1998). In truth, we need a new paradigm for reading instruction regarding wholes and parts. Unlike the chicken and the egg, *both* come first! The whole emphasizes meaning and the natural flow of language. But the parts are equally important for beginning reading.

- Therefore, first-grade teachers may want to begin the school year with the Three-Day Rime Time Routine, then transition into the Five-Day Rime Time Routine by alternating the two for a brief time around mid-year. Move solidly into the Five-Day Rime Time Routine toward the end of the year. This plan allows balanced attention to both the wholes and the parts.

Procedures (adapted from Rasinski & Padak, 2001):

Day 1

1. Introduce the targeted rime.

2. Brainstorm words containing the rime. You may want to begin with one-syllable words. However, as the students gain proficiency, interject multisyllabic words on occasion to demonstrate how these rimes may be used to unlock both small and large words. List the words on chart paper.

3. Read the words with students several times. Have groups and individual students read the words. Encourage students to read the words on their own throughout the day. These word lists can be displayed around the room, so that students may frequently review the words and also use the words in their writing. If wall space is limited, children can record the words into personal spelling dictionaries.

4. Using some of the words from the list that the students brainstormed, pose a Hinky Pinky for the students to solve that contains the rime to be learned. A Hinky Pinky is a riddle for which the answer is two or more rhyming words. For example, what do you call a stone watch? The answer would be a "rock clock."

5. Introduce two or three poems featuring the targeted rime. Poems should be displayed on chart paper or in some way so that all students may easily view them. These poems may be found in poetry books, anthologies, and teacher resource books, or you can easily write them yourself. Granted, it may not win any literary awards, but the following poem for the rime *–ock* was written in under three minutes!

> *Hickory Dickory Dock*
> *I just looked at the clock*
> *It's half past ten*
> *Will my work ever end?*
> *If it did, I might die of shock!*
> *By Belinda Zimmerman*

32
....

CHAPTER 2

*Instructional
Strategies for
Phonics
Development*

Read the poem to the students several times, slightly slower than usual at first and pointing to the words. Students may chime in as they feel comfortable. After a bit, read the poem chorally.

6. Place the students into smaller groups or partners and have them continue to practice reading the poems. Individuals may also volunteer to read the poem aloud to the class.

7. Read and re-read poems, Hinky Pinkies, songs, chants, and other texts that contain the rime. Once the texts have been read and re-read, ask students to find individual words and word parts in the poems. This may be accomplished in a variety of ways. The students may be asked to highlight, point to, underline, or circle the significant words or word parts, especially those containing the targeted rime. You may also want to use a modified fly swatter or Word Whopper to help students identify the targeted words. These may be purchased from educational supply companies or you can easily make your own by cutting a rectangular hole in a new fly swatter. Then you or a student can "whop" one of the words from the poem, and other students are asked to identify it. The Word Whopper isolates the word so that it must be viewed apart from the text that surrounds it. This opportunity for a closer look at the word will help the students recognize it and its component parts when they see it in other reading situations.

8. Ask students to write their own poems that feature the targeted rime. Provide a list of words containing the rimes brainstormed previously in the lesson. Ask students to practice reading and spelling the rimes at home. The sheet also contains the poems practiced during the day so that students can practice reading the poems at home with the support of an adult or more capable reader. At this point, the students take on the role of the poet! Ask students to create a poem that features the targeted rime. Students can write their two- to six-line poems on their own, with a family member, with a classmate, or with a buddy from an upper grade. Rasinski and Padak (2001, p. 54) emphasize:

> This focus on poetry also allows teachers and students to celebrate a wonderful genre that is often neglected and underused in the language arts curriculum and viewed by many teachers as difficult and unfruitful. . . . Even the simple poems that teachers and children may write say something very important to students—"poetry is valued and celebrated in our classroom. We are poets!"

Day 2

1. Begin by having the students copy their poems onto chart paper. The poems will later be hung around the room and used to celebrate reading and writing. This will be described shortly.

2. Next, students read the words and poems from Day 1.

3. Now, it is poetry festival time! In this step, the students go around the room reading and celebrating each new poem written by a classmate. Pausing at each poetry display, the author of the poem has the honor of being the first reader. The job of the first reader is to read the poem aloud, fluently and expressively. Afterward, the first reader may point out key words or call on classmates to point out key words. Then the group reads the poem several times chorally, antiphonally, and finally in pairs and individuals. This provides practice of the targeted rimes in an authentic text while promoting the celebration of language and of the students as authors.

Teaching Tip:

If a parent volunteer, paraprofessional, classroom aide, or even an upper-grade student helper is available, the poems can easily be entered into the computer, printed, and copied for each student to be read again at home. Eventually, students may place these poems into a binder, creating their own classroom anthologies.

Day 3

- Repeat Day 1, targeting a contrasting rime (e.g., *ap, at, ock, ack*).

Day 4

- Repeat Day 2 with the contrasting rime.

Day 5

Day 5 is an opportunity for students to review the rimes of the week and to analyze the differences between the rimes when they occur in the same context.

1. Provide students with a short list of words that contain both rimes that were studied during the week. Students may be asked

34
....

CHAPTER 2

*Instructional
Strategies for
Phonics
Development*

to read the words, spell them, or both. This activity requires students to discriminate the sounds and spelling of the week's rimes in determining the correct word or spelling.

2. Students read a couple poems or texts that contain both rimes studied during the week. Again, this provides students with opportunities to examine both rimes within a common context. If you cannot find poems or other texts, write them yourself or take a dictated text from students, once they understand the lesson routine and the type of text that is desired.

3. Students may take home copies of these poems and be asked to read and reread the texts over the weekend for possible performance on Monday.

Using Rimes to Decode by Analogy

Purpose:

To teach children to use letters, particularly rimes, to infer the pronunciation of an unfamiliar word.

Materials:

Magnetized letters, letter tiles, or letter cards; chart paper or overhead.

Description:

- When teaching students to decode by analogy, assist the children in applying what they already know (i.e., the rime in a familiar or known word family/phonogram word) in order to solve an unknown word containing the same rime.

- Requisite to being able to decode by analogy is the ability to separate words into onsets and rimes and to identify and generate rhyming words. Without this knowledge of how words work, the students will have very limited success with this strategy.

- Students will also need a basic understanding of how the letters in word families represent sounds. Prior to teaching decoding by analogy, provide students with instruction that includes the following (Fox, 2003; Gaskins, Ehri, Cress, O'Hara, & Donnelly, 1997; Juel & Minden-Cupp, 2000):

  1. Phonics instruction in which children learn how the letters that make up rimes represent sounds

  2. Phonemic awareness instruction in separating words into sounds and blending sounds into words

- Decoding by analogy is a helpful strategy for beginning readers, but English has too many rimes for children to rely only on this method of word solving. Knowing the rime *ap* will most certainly help the student to read words such as *sap*, *cap*, and *map*. However, it will not help students unlock words such as *hot*, *play*, and *sit* because these require knowledge of totally different rimes.

Procedures:

Fox (2003, pp. 95–96) advises the following procedures for teaching decoding by analogy:

1. Explicitly teach students how to decode by analogy. The students will benefit from repeated modeling of this process.
   - Draw attention to the rime in a word that they have probably not seen before, such as the *ade* in *shade*. Magnetic letters or letter tiles work well for these demonstrations.
   - Compare the new to the known. Present *shade* next to a known word such as *made*.
   - Remove the /m/ from *made* and in its place substitute the /sh/ in order to spell and say the word *shade*. You may want to say, "See, if you know the word *made*, then you also know *shade*."
2. Introduce clue words. Clue words are Word Wall words or known words that students may refer to when they recognize the rime in the new word. For example, *cat* might be the clue word for the *at* word family. So when the child encounters a new word, the following sequence may occur:
   - The student sees a new word such as *scat* and detects the rime *at* in the new word.
   - The student recalls the clue word for *at*, which is *cat*.
   - The student links the rime in the word *scat* with the clue word *cat* and is able to infer the pronunciation of the new word.

Teaching tip:

The clue words should be on the Word Wall so that students have access to them when reading and writing. Then if a student meets up with a new word such as the word *scat*, the teacher may prompt the student with questions such as, "What word family looks like this one?" or "Can you find a word under the Cc on our Word Wall that has a chunk/word family that looks like this one?" or "If you know *cat*, then you know _____ ."

3. Increase students' reading vocabulary. Students who are able to read greater numbers of words profit more from decoding by analogy than those readers who have only a small corpus of words under control (Wang & Gaffney, 1998). After all, making analogies is about making comparisons. Knowing more words allows the students to generate more comparisons. Conversely, fewer comparisons can be made when fewer words are known.

White Board Word Families

Purpose (adapted from Fox, 2003):

To provide a small group of students with more practice with applying onset/rime knowledge to decode and pronounce words.

Materials:

- Each student will need a white board, a dry erase marker, and a cloth for erasing (may substitute a mini-chalkboard and a sock with a piece of chalk)
- Several sets of colored, laminated 3 × 5 note cards with onsets and rimes.

Description:

In this activity, students combine onsets and rimes to create either real or nonsense words. Determining whether the words are real encourages students to use their speaking vocabularies to cross-check for word meaning. This can be especially helpful for struggling readers since they have a tendency to forego meaning when decoding.

Procedures:

1. Share a word family poem or short story with the small group. For example:

Milk and Cookies

*When you have your milk and cookies
Do you sometimes like to dunk?
Do you eat them at the table,
Or take them to your bunk?
Do you store them in the cupboard,*

Or hide them in a trunk?
When you dip them in your milk,
Do you ever lose a hunk???
(I hate when that happens . . .
it turns my milk to "gunk"!)
By Karen McGuigan Brothers*

2. Have the students locate all of the words from the poem (or story) that contain the same rime. Record the words on a chart as the students locate each one (e.g., *dunk, bunk, trunk, hunk, gunk*). You may also invite the children to think of more words containing the rime and add them to the chart (e.g., *funk, junk, punk, stunk, spunk*).

3. Distribute a white board, a dry erase marker, and an erase cloth to each child in the small group.

4. Explain that the students will be shown a card with a beginning letter (onset) and a card with a word family (rime). Ask students to blend the beginning sound and the word family together to pronounce the word. For example, you may display a /d/ card and an /unk/ card. Students blend the onset and the rime to pronounce the word *dunk*.

5. Next, the students determine whether the pronounced word is a real or nonsense word. You may want to have small groups work together to complete the task a couple of times before calling on individual students.

6. If the word is real, students record it on their dry erase boards. Remind the students that only actual words may be written on the dry erase boards. Since the word *dunk* is indeed a real word, the students will each record this word on their dry erase boards. If you had presented the onset /w/ and the rime /unk/, after blending this into *wunk*, the students would not record *wunk* on their dry erase boards because it is a nonsense word.

7. Figure 2.3 (adapted from Fox, 2003) shows groups of onsets and rimes that can be used to generate both the real and the nonsense words. Groups 1 through 3 are single consonant onsets and simple rimes that form VC short vowel real or nonsense words; groups 4 through 6 consist of onsets and rimes containing consonant clusters and digraphs.

*From Rasinski and Zimmerman (2001, p. 90).

Figure 2.3

Onset-Rime Combinations for White Board Families Activity

Onsets	Rimes
1. p, b, d, r	ig, ug, ag, og, eg
2. h, m, l, f, p	at, id, op, in, et
3. t, m, s, n	ap, ip, et, ub, ot
4. th, ch, gr, sk, sp	in, ip, it, ill, ick
5. thr, cl, tr, cr	ash, amp, ust, ip, ump
6. bl, str, scr, sm, cl	ap, ock, ip, am, uck

Source: Adapted from Fox (2003, p. 115).

Like phonemic awareness, phonics knowledge is a means rather than an end. As you engage students in activities to develop their phonics knowledge, be sure to remind them frequently about the purpose of this instruction. For example, you might say, "Today we have been learning that /ch/ makes the sound that we hear at the beginning of the word *chuckle*. What if you're reading tomorrow and you get stuck on a word that begins with /ch/? What's one thing you know about this word that can help you figure it out?" This sort of prompting can help students remember that they are learning about sound–symbol relationships for the very good reason of assisting their efforts to decode unfamiliar words.

Children's developmental needs should also be part of your thinking as you plan instruction. Ideally, you should determine what children already know and what they need to know to progress as readers. Certainly this will lead to differentiated instruction. It makes no sense to "teach" children about phonics elements with which they are already familiar. Likewise, trying to teach some element that children are not yet ready to learn is frustrating for all involved. Chapter 3 offers some assessment ideas that may help you determine what kinds of phonics instruction will benefit your students.

Finally, while children learn about phonics, it's important to keep the focus on meaning. When decoding unknown words in their reading, children can use phonics and context together. That is, they should learn to check what their phonics knowledge tells them with the sense of what they are reading. They should learn to ask, "What word makes sense here?"

Phonics Materials and Programs

Materials for phonics instruction are abundant. Certainly poetry can provide very effective materials for focusing children's attention on certain phonic elements. The resources listed in Chapter 5 will give you lots of ideas about where to begin looking for these poems. We recommend that you develop a collection, perhaps with colleagues, of poems, songs, jump-rope rhymes, and other examples that you can use to teach phonics.

A great deal of phonics materials are commercially available, as new teacher Kristen, described at the beginning of this chapter, found out. The following questions may help you decide whether a particular program will benefit your students. Or, like Kristen, you can use these questions to see how to supplement or alter materials you are required to use.

- Is the program based on an accurate definition of phonics?
- Is the program intended for a range of developmental levels?
- Will children find the activities engaging?
- Is the amount of time per day appropriate?
- Are suggestions for instruction as well as practice provided? Do the practice activities provide the kind of scaffolding children need in order to learn? Will students be able to complete practice activities independently?
- Is the overall instructional routine appropriate?
- Are high-utility phonic elements stressed?
- Is skill instruction connected to authentic texts?
- Are assessment ideas offered?

Professional Development Suggestions

Work with two or three other teachers, ideally those at your own grade level. First, make your own notes about each of the questions that follows. Then discuss the questions with your colleagues. See if you can reach consensus. Make notes about your ideas and questions. Finally, share your ideas with the whole group.

- How can we evaluate the usefulness of our current materials for phonics instruction?

  _____

  _____

  _____

  _____

  _____

  _____

- How much phonics instruction should be whole group? Small group? Individual? Why?

  _____

  _____

  _____

  _____

  _____

  _____

- Revisit the semantic feature analysis that you completed at the beginning of the chapter. Now consider the strategies presented in this chapter as well as discussions you may have had with colleagues. Revise the chart, and tell your colleagues about why you have made these changes.

  _____

  _____

  _____

  _____

  _____

  _____

- How can we determine what children already know about phonics and what they need to know? What kind of information, if any, would be helpful to obtain from children's previous teachers? What kind of information, if any, should we share with children's future teachers?

_____

_____

_____

_____

_____

_____

- How can we explain phonics to parents?

_____

_____

_____

_____

_____

CHAPTER 3

Assessing Phonics Development

Big Ideas

In each of the books in this series, we have identified several "big ideas" to guide your thinking about assessment. These big ideas apply to assessing all aspects of literacy learning (indeed, to all learning), but the comments and examples below frame them in the context of assessing children's phonics knowledge and abilities—that is, what they know about sound–symbol relationships and how they put that knowledge to work in their reading.

- *Focus on critical information.* Any assessment is most efficient and effective if it is focused. In planning assessments for phonics, then, you will want to aim for a direct connection between what you need to know and the assessment tools/strategies you use. In the area of phonics knowledge and ability, decisions about what you need to know are somewhat dependent on your grade level and your students' abilities, but this description of the decoding process may help you decide:

  > When we ask students to apply their phonics skills to reading a word that is unfamiliar to them in its printed form, we are actually asking them to use an array of language knowledge and processes: knowledge of the alphabetic principle and how it works (spoken words are represented by written spellings); knowledge and use of letter-sound correspondences; skill in blending graphemes into phonemes; knowledge and use of syllabication and accent if the word is multisyllabic; and use of metacognition to compare the word to real words. If the word is in connected text, we also want them to use context cues to see if it makes sense in relation to the surrounding words and ideas. (Calhoun, 2004, p. 123)

  This description points to the underlying complexity involved in "sounding it out." At the very least, thinking about three different aspects of the structure of knowledge may be helpful: factual knowledge (e.g., letter–sound relationships), skills (ability to decode, ability to apply "fix-up" strategies), and principles and generalizations (e.g., we read to make meaning, what we read is supposed to make sense) (McTighe & Wiggins, 2004).
  It may also help to think about a student whose phonics abilities are very strong. Try making a list of his or her observable indicators: What would he or she do? Say? What would you see or hear that shows phonics strengths? Having thought

about the abstract definition and your own students, then, you can decide what critical information to focus on for assessment. McTighe and Wiggins (2004) suggest that this process works best when it begins at the end: (1) if the desired result is for learners to . . . (2) then assessment should provide you with evidence of . . . and (3) so assessment tasks need to include something like. . . .

- *Look for patterns of behavior.* Rob Tierney (1998) notes that assessment "should be viewed as ongoing and suggestive, rather than fixed or definitive" (p. 385). No single instance can possibly tell you what you need to know about a child's phonics abilities. Tasks can certainly affect children's ability to show what they know, for example. A text that is too easy offers no decoding opportunities, whereas a too-difficult text may "short-circuit" a child's abilities.

  Your assessment goal should be to determine patterns of behavior that show phonics skills and abilities. To do this, you need a plan. Get baseline information about children at the beginning of the year. Then select a few children to focus on each week. Some of this will be routine, but you may also want to select children about whom you need more information or children whose current behavior is surprising in some way (Rasinski & Padak, 2004).

- *Recognize developmental progressions (can't, can sometimes, can always) and children's cultural or linguistic differences.* Tierney (1998) advises that "assessment should be more developmental and sustained than piecemeal and shortsighted" (p. 384). "I envision . . . assessments that build upon, recognize, and value rather than displace what students have experienced in their worlds" (p. 381). Your plans should be sensitive to both of these issues.

  Developmental progressions in phonics may mean that a child's ability to use some bit of graphophonic knowledge is uneven for a time—sometimes but not other times the child is able to use the knowledge successfully. This "can sometimes" stage often means that the learning is in process. Likewise, when you are sure that a child knows and can use some bit of information, you will no longer need to assess this aspect of phonics ability. This means that the focus of your assessment will likely change over the course of the school year. Good record-keeping will enable you to keep assessments streamlined and focused on children about whom you have questions.

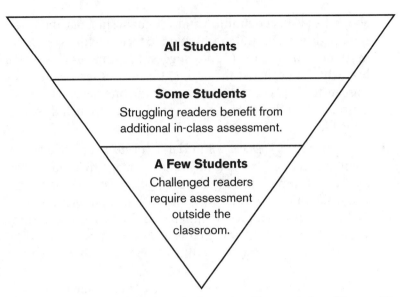

All Students

Some Students
Struggling readers benefit from
additional in-class assessment.

A Few Students
Challenged readers
require assessment
outside the
classroom.

Source: Rasinski and Padak (2004, p. 277). Reprinted by permission of Pearson Education, Inc.

Cultural or linguistic differences may influence some aspects of children's phonics performance. Children who are learning English, for example, may have first language phonology that differs from English, and this can affect their performance on assessment tasks. Knowing about these differences can help ensure that your assessments yield useful information.

- *Be parsimonious.* The question: How much assessment information do you need? The answer: Enough to make good instructional decisions. One way to conceptualize this quantity-of-information question is to think in terms of three related layers of assessment information, as shown above.

At the top of the figure is what is done for and with all students in the class. Begin with a broad plan to assess children's phonics ability at the beginning of the year and then, perhaps, quarterly. Remember that you probably won't need to assess all children in all skill areas as the school year progresses because learning will take place. That is, when someone knows long /e/, for example, and you know that the child knows it, there's no longer a need to assess this bit of phonic knowledge.

Then think about results: What (or who) do you still have questions about? This is the point to move to the second layer of the triangle. Here you will do more focused (and time-consuming) phonics assessments. You might work individually with a child, perhaps more of what you've already done or a "deeper" assessment. If you still have questions, don't hesitate to ask for outside help. A child or two in the class may benefit from a diagnosis by a reading specialist or other highly specialized professional. Don't delay and don't hesitate. Every lost day represents lost opportunities for that child's learning. Above all, keep assessments at these different layers related to one another, focused on the same key issues. To do otherwise might lead to confusion rather than clarification.

- *Use instructional situations for assessment purposes.* Tierney (1998) notes that ideally, "assessments should emerge from the classroom rather than be imposed upon it" (p. 375). We can think of two good reasons for this stance, one conceptual and the other practical. From a conceptual perspective, you want to know how children behave in typical instructional situations. After all, a major purpose of assessment is to provide instructional guidance. In terms of phonics assessment, "typical instructional situations" may mean looking at a child's ability to decode real words (not nonsense words) in the context of real reading. Such a focus would allow you to understand the child's ability to coordinate strategies and to put knowledge to use, both important aspects of decoding ability.

  From a practical standpoint, gathering assessment information from instruction saves time for your teaching and children's learning. Children don't learn much of value during testing sessions. To evaluate your phonics instruction for possible assessment situations, you might begin by listing instructional routines that focus on phonics: When and how do you ordinarily work with children on phonics issues? When do children have opportunities to use their phonics knowledge? Then develop a plan to capture observations about what children know and can do during instruction. This may be as simple as preparing an observation chart (see page 50) for making brief notes. Above all, take Karen West's (1998) advice to heart: "I want instruction and evaluation to be in meaningful authentic contexts" (p. 550).

- *Include plans for (1) using assessment information to guide instruction and (2) sharing assessment information with children and their parents.* The last step of your assessment planning might be to double-check ideas against their primary purpose: to help you teach more effectively. You will also want to think about how to share assessment information with your students and their parents. With regard to the former, it may be particularly important to think about how you can adjust instruction for both children who need more phonics instruction and children who have mastered these concepts and are ready for different instruction. Grouping for instruction will probably be necessary, so you will want to think about the management issues associated with particular grouping patterns for young children.

Moreover, consider how you can share assessment information with children and their parents. Knowing that they are making progress will keep children engaged in their learning. And parents, of course, are both interested in their children's progress in school and frequently willing to assist in their children's education. Indeed, many phonics practice activities can be developed to be game-like and therefore perfect for at-home suggestions for parents. Rob Tierney (1998) reminds us that it's important to keep parents informed, but more than that, involved: "Rather than keep the parent or caregiver at arm's length . . . , we need to embrace the concerns that parents have and the contributions they can make" (p. 380).

Evaluate Your Current Assessment Practices

The chart on page 49 will help you take a careful look at your current assessment practices in phonics. To complete the chart, first list all the ways you currently assess students' phonics skills and abilities in the "Assessment Tool/ Strategy" column. Then consider the information each tool or strategy provides about each of the critical aspects by marking the chart: + = excellent source of information; – = some information; blank = no information. When the chart is complete, make plans for revision. Are some critical aspects receiving too much/not enough attention? Can some tools/strategies be eliminated or revised? What revisions will enhance your overall assessment strategies?

Ideas for Assessment

What did you conclude by analyzing your current strategies for phonics assessment? Perhaps you are satisfied that you have enough of the right kind of information about your students. If not, you may find some of the following ideas helpful for supplementing your plans.

Critical Aspects: Phonics Instruction

Assessment Tool/Strategy	Awareness of Difficulty (e.g., knows when an unknown word is encountered)	Knowledge of Letter-Sound Correspondences	Skill in Applying Phonics Knowledge	Ability to Check for Meaning (e.g., makes sure sounded-out word makes sense in text)	Other Notes

Notes about revisions: _____

_____

Observation Chart

You can create a chart (see page 50) to use when children show their phonics abilities. You can make brief notes on the chart or use some kind of symbol system, such as A = Advanced, S = Secure, D = Developing, and N = Not Observed. Since assessing children in this way once every month or two may provide enough information, you can focus on different students each week and, over time, observe all your students.

Observation Chart

Indicator	Child's Name ___	Child's Name ___	Child's Name ___	Child's Name ___
Awareness of difficulty				
Knowledge of letter–sound correspondences				
Skill in applying phonics knowledge				
Ability to check for meaning				

Rimes Assessment

Rimes (or phonograms or word families) are the parts of syllables that contain the vowel and the letters that follow. Common rimes are listed in the chart on page 51 along with one-syllable and multisyllable words containing them (Rasinski & Padak, 2001). You can ask children to read the words in lists or on cards, or you can put them into simple sentences (e.g., for –*ay*: Say, "Will you be my playmate?"). Make note of errors or patterns of error that occur, and use this information to help you decide what the child needs to learn next.

Unaided Writing

Children learn about written language, including phoneme–grapheme (sound–symbol) relationships, gradually. Most scholars believe that the overall learning process involves generating and testing hypotheses—in essence trying something out and then checking the results. One of the best ways to see phonics learning through this lens is by analyzing children's unaided writing. To spell an unfamiliar word, the child needs to think about its sounds and represent them with letters. By examining these inventions, you can learn about the child's understanding of sound–symbol relationships.

Common One-Syllable and Multisyllable Rimes

Rime	1 Syllable	Multisyllable	Notes
-ay	Say	Playmate	
-ill	Spill	Willful	
-ip	Ship	Skipping	
-at	Bat	Satisfy	
-am	Slam	Hamster	
-ag	Brag	Shaggy	
-ack	Stack	Packer	
-ank	Crank	Blanket	
-ick	Quick	Cricket	
-ell	Yell	Shellfish	
-ot	Got	Hotcake	
-ing	King	Stacking	
-ap	Clap	Kidnap	
-unk	Junk	Bunker	
-ail	Nail	Railroad	
-ain	Chain	Mainstay	
-eed	Weed	Seedling	
-y	Try	Myself	
-out	Spout	Without	
-ug	Bug	Dugout	
-op	Stop	Popcorn	
-in	Chin	Tinsel	
-an	Stan	Flannel	
-est	Nest	Chester	
-ink	Think	Trinket	
-ow	Grow	Snowflake	
-ew	Chew	Newest	
-ore	Score	Adore	
-ed	Red	Bedtime	
-ab	Crab	Dabble	
-ob	Knob	Robber	
-ock	Block	Jockey	
-ake	Brake	Remake	
-ine	Shine	Porcupine	
-ight	Light	Sighted	
-im	Brim	Swimming	
-uck	Stuck	Truckload	
-um	Chum	Drummer	

You can examine students' unaided writing, perhaps monthly, and keep track of your observations. To do this, select two or three writing samples from the month. Look particularly at the child's inventions for evidence of phonics knowledge. If you see several instances of use of a phonic element, make note of the possible learning. Note that you are assessing phonics knowledge, not spelling. For example, Ben wrote

My favrit annumel is a porcepin becaus he has nedls.

My, is, a, he, and *has* may be sight words and aren't useful for thinking about Ben's phonics knowledge. Look at the inventions: Does Ben know that the sound /n/ is represented by the letter *n*? How do you know? This is the kind of analysis that yields a list of phonic elements that a student may know. Then, if you also see this phonic knowledge used the next month, you can be sure the child knows that particular sound–symbol relationship.

Quick Oral Reading Assessments

Take note of how a child handles unknown words during instructional oral reading—for example during a reading conference or when the child is selecting a new book to read. This will allow you to capture important information about phonics abilities and the extent to which a child knows that the word he or she says should (1) match the text visually ("look right") and (2) make sense in the context of the text. You can use Running Record (Clay, 1993) procedures or a simple coding system to keep track of the child's errors or miscues: (1) for substitutions, write what the child said on top of the text word(s), (2) for omissions, cross out the text, (3) for insertions, use the editor's carat (^), and (4) for corrections, use ©.

When you have gathered several samples of a child's reading, you can analyze miscues by comparing them to words in the text. For each pair (i.e., miscue and text word), you can ask questions such as:

- Do they look the same in the beginning, middle, and end?
- Do they sound the same in the beginning, middle, and end?
- Are they the same part of speech?
- Are their meanings similar?
- Does the child try to correct miscues that change meaning? How successful is he or she?

You may want to make notes about your analysis to include in a child's reading portfolio. Be sure to date the notes and include the title of the text. Over all, though, use your analysis to answer the question: What does this child do when she or he encounters an unknown word? Then use your answer to this question to guide instruction.

Plans for Change

In this chapter you have evaluated your own assessment strategies for phonics and, as a result, perhaps generated some ideas for change. Use the chart on the next page to make notes about the changes you wish to make. As you do so, make sure that these changes reflect the "big ideas" outlined at the beginning of the section:

- Focus on critical information.
- Look for patterns of behavior.
- Recognize developmental progressions and attend to cultural differences.
- Be parsimonious. (Which of your strategies will work for all of your students? Which might be reserved for more careful attention to some students' phonics abilities?)
- Get assessment information from instruction as much as possible.

You may want to share your plans with others to get their feedback.

Planning: Phonics Assessment

Goal _____

Plans by _____ Date _____

Action Steps: What do I need to do?	Materials/Resources	Evaluation: How will I assess the usefulness of this change?

CHAPTER 4

Fostering Home-School Connections

*I*n earlier chapters, we explored how children acquire letter–sound relationships and decoding skills and the best instructional strategies for supporting that process. In this chapter, we will consider issues that go "beyond strategies." In particular, we address English language learners (ELLs) and provide guidelines and suggestions for at-home phonics activities.

English Language Learners and Phonics Development

Did you ever study a foreign language in school? If so, you may recall feeling both excited and confused as you explored a whole new way of talking and thinking. This is how many children from other cultures feel as they enter U.S. classrooms. Given the cultural and linguistic diversity of the nation's population, your classroom may have children from several countries. How do you plan instruction that reaches each individual learner?

It is important to keep in mind that children raised in bilingual homes have unique advantages as well as unique challenges. These children bring rich background experiences that can be tapped to enhance everyone's learning. They know how to move between two languages, integrating sounds and meanings into new words and grammatical structures. Their natural manipulation of two languages promotes higher-level thinking. Yet, ELL students sometimes feel lost in the unfamiliar linguistic and academic world in which they find themselves. Fitzgerald and Graves (2004) describe this feeling:

> Many English-language learners bring an array of emotions to our classrooms that often are not evident on the surface. The student who is afraid that his talk will sound funny to others may hide his self-consciousness. The student who does not fully understand what is said may hold a steady gaze and outwardly appear confident or even cocky. (p. 3)

Fortunately, everything we have learned so far about how to teach phonics applies to both first and second language learners: ELL students need an understanding of the alphabetic principle, letter–sound relationships, and opportunities to develop word-identification strategies such as word solving by analogy and having the students write what they hear. The major difference is that ELLs may require more scaffolding and practice. Following are three key ideas to keep in mind as you plan instruction for second language learners.

- *Build conceptual connections through prior knowledge.* Teachers know that activating and applying prior knowledge is central to all learning: As students compare new information with what they already know, they deepen their understanding of a topic. Second language learners, however, may lack basic content or conceptual knowledge in the texts teachers ask them to read. Meaning is one of the cueing systems students use when attempting to decode unfamiliar words. If ELLs have a limited understanding of the semantics of English, accessing meaning cues during word solving is quite challenging, to say the least. Building oral language skills is critical for success here. You can use discussion to relate unfamiliar topics or concepts to similar topics or concepts in ELL students' lives. It is also helpful to teach ELLs to read using culturally familiar materials and patterned, predictable text to build sight vocabularies, reinforce English language patterns, and anticipate sentence structure. In addition, it may be helpful to preteach some vocabulary that is central to understanding the text so that the student is not put into the position of sounding out every unknown word that is encountered.

- *Begin phonics instruction early.* Kindergarten and first grade are ideal times to formally teach phonics because children are expected to acquire word identification strategies during this time. Phonics and decoding are essential to the process of word identification. You can expect gains from your students in decoding, word recognition, comprehension, and fluency when beginning readers, particularly ELLs, receive early, intensive, targeted, and sustained phonics instruction over an extended period of time (Fox, 2008; Gunn, Smolkowski, Biglan, & Black, 2002; Rasinski & Padak, 2001). As with all learners, ELL students need plenty of opportunities to apply their budding phonics understandings while spelling, writing, and reading. With this type of early instruction and support, there is a greater likelihood that ELLs will achieve on-grade-level status by the close of grade 2 (Lesaux & Siegel, 2003). Thus, the case for starting early with phonics instruction cannot be overstated.

- *Flexibly group students for phonics instruction.* It may be surprising to learn that native English speakers and ELLs follow a similar learning sequence when learning letter–sound patterns (Chiappe, Siegel, & Wade-Wooley, 2002). Although the sequence of learning may be similar, the rate of learning is often a bit slower for the ELL students. It may be tempting to think that the reading needs of ELLs would be best met if the students were placed in small homogenous ELL groups. However, just the opposite is recommended. Fox (2008) suggests that teachers group ELLs with native English speakers in small groups according to their progress and ability in learning and applying phonics. Students may be exited from the group as they achieve greater mastery over the phonics elements and word-solving strategies presented. It should be noted that it is not unusual for ELLs to experience a slightly extended stay in the group due to the slower pace of ELL phonics learning.

Communicating with Families

Both practitioners and researchers have long recognized the importance of parental involvement in children's early reading achievement. Children whose families encourage at-home literacy activities have higher phonemic awareness and decoding skills (Burgess, 1999), higher reading achievement in the elementary grades (Cooter, Marrin, & Mills-House, 1999), and advanced oral language development (Senechal, LeFevre, & Thomas, 1998). Family literacy professionals often point out that parents are their children's first and most important teachers. Instructing parents to simply "read to your child" may be a start, but it is not enough. Parents need specific suggestions and guidelines about what to do and how to respond to their child's literacy development. In this section we offer guidelines and some sample activities for home involvement programs and practices that foster children's phonics development.

Teachers know that home involvement can provide rich opportunities for children to develop as readers. Moreover, it's important for children to see reading and literacy activities as worthwhile and critical outside of school as well as within school walls. Yet, home involvement programs are sometimes frustrating for teachers, parents, and children alike. Our work with supporting home involvement programs has led us to several design characteristics. These must be present for home involvement programs for young readers to be successful (Rasinski & Padak, 2004):

- *Use proven and effective strategies.* Many parents have limited time to devote to working with their children, so at-home activities must be focused on ideas that have been proven to make a positive difference in children's reading achievement.

- *Use authentic reading texts.* Reading aloud to children allows parents to model fluent reading as well as point out text features. Similarly, when parents read with their children or listen to their children read, children grow as readers. These simple activities—read to, read with, and listen to children—are powerful ways to promote reading achievement. What about texts? We believe it's essential for them to be authentic. For young readers, texts such as simple poems, song lyrics, jokes, or jump-rope rhymes work very well. In addition to authenticity, these texts often feature onsets and rimes (word families).

- *Provide materials.* Some parent involvement plans fail because parents lack appropriate texts or the time or resources to acquire them. The easiest solution is to provide parents and children with reading materials. In addition to looking for materials in books, teachers will find the Internet a treasure trove of wonderful materials for children and parents to read. (See resources listed in Chapter 5 for examples.)

With these principles in mind, you can develop some simple home phonics activities. Suggestions include the following:

- Applying decoding skills is a problem-solving process. Talk to parents about the importance of allowing their child time to analyze when the child pauses at an unknown word rather than automatically supplying the word whenever the child is "stuck." It is also beneficial to provide parents with several prompts that they can use to encourage the child to engage in the problem solving. Parents have a tendency to over-rely on the age-old prompt, "Sound it out," so it is helpful for teachers to provide the parents with some more effective alternatives such as:

"Get your mouth ready for the beginning sound."
"What letter do you see at the beginning (or end) of the word? What sound does it stand for?"
Ask the child to pronounce the first sound in a word and then say, "Now that you have the first sound, say more of that word."
If the unknown word contains a familiar word part (phonogram), the parent might say, "There's a part in this word that you know. Use your fingers to frame the part of the word you know. Then you might be able to get the word on your own."

"Can you think of a word that would make sense here and begins with these letters?"

- Encourage parents to make trips to the local library a regular part of their routine. Emphasize that in order to do something well, time must be devoted to it. You may have heard the saying, "Whatever you put your energy toward grows." Professional football players certainly do not become star athletes by watching football on television. They become skilled because they spend a great deal of time playing and practicing the game. The process of becoming a successful reader is no exception. Thus, it is crucial that parents and children have access to quality children's literature and that time is spent each day enjoying this rich literature and practicing reading appropriate texts. Predictable books such as *Brown Bear, Brown Bear* by Bill Martin are especially helpful with young and/or struggling readers because they are designed to repeat certain high-frequency words. Multiple exposures to certain words help children to commit these words to memory. See Chapter 5 for a list of patterned, predictable texts.

- Talk with parents about the importance of having their children have fun with words. Parents can encourage word play at home by placing plastic, magnetic letters on the refrigerator or a cookie sheet. The children can manipulate the magnetic letters to generate lists of rhyming words or to form words that begin (or end) with a particular sound.

- Show parents how to do paired reading with their children. Applying phonics skills requires that children look closely at print. Parents will want to encourage their child to point to the words as he or she is reading. Pointing to the words forces the eyes to look more closely at each word, which increases the likelihood that the child will learn and remember the word. The parent may also informally ask questions about the words encountered during the reading. Rasinski and Padak (2001) caution that reading to and with the child should continue to be an occasion for parent–child bonding rather than a formal reading lesson. Nonetheless, pointing to the words, drawing a bit of attention to word meanings, and discussing the text may accelerate the child's literacy development and reduce some of the difficulty many beginning readers experience as they learn to recognize and analyze words.

- Gentry (2006) reminds us that reading and writing are related processes and that we must give provide children with many occasions to do both so that we may take advantage of this reciprocal relationship. The process of writing allows children an opportunity to apply emerging phonics knowledge. Parents can facilitate both reading and writing development by encouraging their children to write at home. Supplies for writing should be accessible to the child. Activities such as making grocery store and "to do" lists, creating recipes and menus, and keeping journals or diaries provide fun and meaningful opportunities to read and write for real purposes.

- You may want to inform parents that recent research has shown that children who view television that contains captions improve their word learning and their overall reading (Adler, 1985; Koskinen et al., 1987; Koskinen, Wilson, Gambrell, & Neuman, 1993; Neuman & Koskinen, 1992). Viewing the words on screen while simultaneously hearing them assists readers in both word identification and fluency. The parent should talk to the child about how "reading the screen" during television viewing can improve reading. Rasinski and Padak (2001) point out that some children find the captions distracting and bothersome at first, but the child usually becomes comfortable with the process after just a couple of days.

- You may want to explain to parents how to play a fun word guessing game called "Read My Mind" (Cunningham & Allington, 1994; Gentry, 2006). The parents may find it beneficial to play this game using words from the child's weekly spelling list. In this activity, children are asked to number a sheet of paper from 1 to 5. The parent selects a secret word from the list and then provides the child with clues that will highlight phonic elements such as beginning letters, word families, vowel patterns rhymes, or semantic and syntactic clues. The child writes a guess down after each clue is given. The same guess may be written more than once as long as it fits the given clues. After five clues, the child should have correctly guessed the word. For example, if the secret word is *friend*, the parent may offer clues such as:

My secret word has six letters.
My secret word has one syllable.
My secret word begins with consonant cluster.
My secret word rhymes with the word *end*.
My secret word means the same thing as buddy or pal.

In Conclusion

This chapter has addressed issues related to working with children who are learning English (ELLs) and provided ideas for home–school involvement. English language learners will learn phonics and decoding in much the same ways as their native English-speaking classmates. They may need more time and, especially, more of teacher support to do so.

Rasinski and Padak (2001, p. 204) have characterized parental involvement and home–school connections as the "secret weapon" in learning to read. For most children, especially those struggling in the area of reading, home support that takes the form of the recommendations suggested in this chapter may be the variable that makes the difference between reading progress and failure. In fact, a research study of second- and eighth-grade students' reading achievement showed that parental involvement, support, and the amount of time children spent at home reading were the most powerful factors associated with student achievement (Postlethwaite & Ross, 1992). Thus, any exemplary program designed to improve students' reading progress, fluency, and word recognition must include a parent/home support component (Rasinski & Padak, 2001).

Professional Development Suggestions

Book Club

Discuss the following with a small group of colleagues. Make notes about your decisions (and questions or concerns, if any). Plan to share your ideas with others in your professional development group.

1. How can poetry help you help children learn about onsets, rimes, rhymes, and other word-related issues? Work together to develop some word study routines that involve poetry.

2. How much word study instruction should be whole-group oriented? How much should be small-group oriented? What kinds of groups? How much individual work? And for all of the above, why?

3. Think of the ELL students you currently teach. How can you determine what they already know about the sound–symbol system in English?

4. Read the following vignette and, with your colleagues, discuss the questions that follow.

VIGNETTE

When you receive your class list in the summer, you are delighted to learn that several children who have been identified as "gifted" will be in your second-grade class. You spend the last couple of weeks of the summer gathering challenging phonics activities with these children in mind. Your goal, as you put it to some friends, is to "revise the curriculum to their level."

After a few weeks of school, you conclude that some of the "gifted" students simply seem to be well-behaved kids who do what is asked of them. They don't seem to be particularly creative or perceptive, and they appear to lack age-appropriate decoding skills. Other "gifted" students, however, do seem to be both perceptive and creative. Their reading abilities astonish you. Your challenging activities don't challenge them at all.

You seek advice from colleagues. One suggests that students spend much of their reading time pursuing independent projects. Another maintains that, gifted or not, students must complete all the phonics (and other language arts) activities because it's likely that they have "missed some skills." A third advises you to "leave them alone. Those bright kids don't need us as much as the children who are reading below grade level."

QUESTIONS

- Should teachers be concerned about determining gifted/talented students' needs in reading? Why?
- How should a teacher determine children's needs in phonics?
- Is it possible for students to "miss some skills"? Why?
- What type of decoding instruction makes sense for primary-level children who are reading well above grade level?

5. In the Principals' FAQ Project (Mraz et al., 2001), principals provided questions about phonics and decoding that parents frequently asked. The questions are listed here. Use what you have learned throughout this professional development program to compile responses to the questions.

- What is phonics?
- How do phonics awareness activities help my child learn to read?
- What's the relationship among phonemic awareness, phonics, and writing development?

6. Complete one or both of the following charts with your insights and plans for phonics instruction.

Curriculum Alignment—Phonics

Component	What Is . . .	What Should Be . . .
Curriculum		
Instruction		
Materials		
Assessment		
Home Connection		

Source: Adapted from Taylor and Collins (2003).

Goal Planning—Phonics

Goal _____

Plans by _____ Date _____

Action Steps: What do I need to do?	Materials/Resources	Evaluation: How will I assess the usefulness of this change?

CHAPTER 5

Resources

*I*n this final chapter, we offer resources for classroom activities and for your own further learning. Both print and Web-based resources are provided.

Websites

Websites for Word Study

Kids' Crosswords and Other Puzzles: www.kidcrosswords.com

Crosswords, word searches, crostics, and other word games.

Puzzle Choice: www.puzzlechoice.com/pc/Kids_Choicex.html

Lots of puzzles at this site—crosswords, word searches, word play, and more.

Puzzles by Puzzability: www.puzzability.com/puzzles/

Word games of all sorts that change regularly.

Vocabulary University: www.vocabulary.com/

Full of puzzles and other activities based on Greek and Latin roots. The puzzles change regularly.

Word Games and Puzzles!: http://mindfun.com/

Calls itself the "Web's best spot for online trivia games, word puzzles and quizzes!" Students will find word scrambles, webs, crossword puzzles—even Boggle. Lots of word trivia too!

Websites for Phonics Fun

Phonics Interactivities/Memory Matching Game: www.sadlier-oxford .com/phonics/control_pagefront2.htm.

Here, the kids are asked to match pairs of rhyming words.

Between the Lions from PBS Kids: www.pbskids.org.lions/games/

Play games with words and learn spelling from fun characters.

Gamequarium/Free Phonics Games: www.gamequarium.com/phonics28.html

This site allows you to customize games for your students.

Phonics Games—Free to Print and Play: www.adrianbruce.com/reading/ games.htm

A collection of free phonics and word games available for downloading and printing.

BBC Schools—Words and Pictures: www.bbc.co.uk/schools/ wordsandpictures/

Colorful games, printable pages, animations, and other activities to help 5- to 7-year-olds with reading and phonics.

Softschools—Free Phonics Worksheets and Games: www.softschools.com/language_arts/phonics/

> Free phonics games, flashcards, and online activities for kids, including short vowel sounds and long vowel sounds for preschoolers and kindergartners.

Clifford Interactive Storybooks: www.teacher.scholastic.com/clifford1/

> Interactive storybooks featuring Clifford The Big Red Dog plus phonics fun, games, and stories for early readers.

Literacy Center Phonics: www.literacycenter.net

> Teaches letter formations and letter sounds in English, Spanish, French, and German.

Phonics Game Show: www.surfnetkids.com/quiz/phonics

> With a Jeopardy-like game board, students are quizzed about certain phonics rules and other aspects of decoding and the alphabetic principle.

Trade Books to Enhance Phonics Instruction

The list of books that follows was adapted from Trachtenburg (1990).

Short a

Flack, M. *Angus and the Cat.* Doubleday, 1931.
Griffith, H. *Alex and the Cat.* Greenwillow, 1982.
Kent, J. *The Fat Cat.* Scholastic. 1971.
Most, B. *There's an Ant in Anthony.* William Morrow, 1980.
Nodset, J. *Who Took the Farmer's Hat?* Harper & Row, 1963.
Robins, J. *Addie Meets Max.* Harper & Row, 1985.
Schmidt, K. *The Gingerbread Man.* Scholastic, 1985.

Long a

Aardema, V. *Bringing the Rain to Kapiti Plain.* Dial, 1981.
Bang, M. *The Paper Crane.* Greenwillow, 1985.
Byars, B. *The Lace Snail.* Viking, 1975.
Henkes, K. *Sheila Rae, the Brave.* Greenwillow, 1987.
Hines, A. *Taste the Raindrops.* Greenwillow, 1983.

Short and Long a

Aliki. *Jack and Jake.* Greenwillow, 1986.
Slobodkina, E. *Caps for Sale.* Addison-Wesley, 1940.

Short *e*

Ets, M. H. *Elephant in a Well*. Viking, 1972.
Galdone, P. *The Little Red Hen*. Scholastic, 1973.
Ness, E. *Yeck Eck*. E. P. Dutton, 1974.
Schecter, B. *Hester the Jester*. Harper & Row, 1977.
Thayer, J. *I Don't Believe in Elves*. William Morrow, 1975.
Wing, H. R. *Ten Pennies for Candy*. Holt, Rinehart and Winston, 1963.

Long *e*

Galdone, P. *Little Bo-Peep*. Clarion/Ticknor & Fields. 1986.
Keller, H. *Ten Sleepy Sheep*. Greenwillow, 1983.
Martin, B. *Brown Bear, Brown Bear, What Do You See?* Henry Holt, 1967.
Oppenheim, J. *Have You Seen Trees?* Young Scott Books, 1967.
Soule, J. *Never Tease A Weasel*. Parent's Magazine Press, 1964.
Thomas, P. *"Stand Back," said the Elephant, "I'm Going to Sneeze!"* Lothrop, Lee, & Shepard, 1971.

Short *i*

Ets, M. H. *Gilberto and the Wind*. Viking, 1966.
Hutchins, P. *Titch*. Macmillan, 1971.
Keats, E. J. *Whistle for Willie*. Viking, 1964.
Lewis, T. P. *Call for Mr. Sniff*. Harper & Row, 1981.
Lobel, A. *Small Pig*. Harper & Row, 1969.
McPhail, D. *Fix-It*. E. P. Dutton, 1984.
Patrick, G. *This is . . . .* Carolrhoda, 1970.
Robins, J. *My Brother, Will*. Greenwillow, 1986.

Long *i*

Berenstain, S., & Berenstain, J. *The Bike Lesson*. Random House, 1964.
Cameron, J. *If Mice Could Fly*. Atheneum, 1979.
Cole, S. *When the Tide Is Low*. Lothrop, Lee & Shepard, 1985.
Gelman, R. *Why Can't I Fly?* Scholastic, 1976.
Hazen, B. S. *Tight Times*. Viking, 1979.

Short *o*

Benchley, N. *Oscar Otter*. Harper & Row, 1966.
Dunrea, O. *Mogwogs on the March!* Holiday House, 1985.
Emberley, B. *Drummer Hoff*. Prentice-Hall, 1967.

McKissack, P. *Flossie & the Fox*. Dial, 1986.

Miller, P., & Seligman, I. *Big Frogs, Little Frogs*. Holt, Rinehart and Winston, 1963.

Rice, E. *"The Frog and the Ox"* from *Once in a Wood*. Greenwillow, 1979.

Seuss, Dr. *Fox in Socks*. Random House, 1965.

Long o

Cole, B. *The Giant's Toe*, Farrar, Strauss, & Giroux, 1986.

Gerstein, M. *Roll Over!* Crown, 1984.

Johnston, T. *The Adventures of Mole and Troll*. G. P. Putnam's Sons, 1972.

Shulevitz, U. *One Monday Morning*. Charles Scribner's Sons, 1967.

Tresselt, A. *White Snow, Bright Snow*. Lothrop, Lee, & Shepard, 1947.

Short u

Carroll, R. *Where's the Bunny?* Henry Z. Walck, 1950.

Cooney, N. E. *Donald Says Thumbs Down*. G. P. Putnam's Sons, 1987.

Friskey, M. *Seven Little Ducks*. Children's Press. 1940.

Lorenz, L. *Big Gus and Little Gus*. Prentice-Hall, 1982.

Marshall, J. *The Cut-Ups*. Viking Kestrel, 1984.

Udry, J. M. *Thump and Plunk*. Harper & Row, 1981.

Yashima, T. *Umbrella*. Viking Penguin, 1958.

Long u

Lobel, A. *The Troll Music*. Harper & Row, 1966.

Segal, L. *Tell Me a Trudy*. Farrar, Strauss, & Giroux, 1977.

Slobodkin, L. *"Excuse Me—Certainly!"* Vanguard Press, 1959.

Predictable Books

Predictable books make use of rhyme, repetition of words, phrases, sentences, refrains, and such patterns as cumulative structure and turn-around plots. These stories invite children to make predictions or guesses about words, phrases, sentences, events, and characters that could come next in the story (Simpson, 1986). Anticipating text in this way positively influences the development of all of the big five areas of reading: *phonemic awareness, phonics, fluency, vocabulary*, and *comprehension*. In addition, reading predictable texts is pleasurable for children. The more predictable the story, the greater the likelihood that children will enjoy, recall, and reread the story again and again.

The following are short descriptions of the eight types of predictable texts (Cochrane, 1984):

Categories of Predictable Books

1. *Repetitive.* The same phrase, sentence, or story scenario repeats throughout the story.

2. *Cumulative.* Each time a new event occurs, all previous events in the story are repeated. In other words, each part repeats the previous part and then a new part is added.

3. *Rhythm/Rhyme Sequence.* Rhyming words, refrains, or patterns are used and repeated throughout the story.

4. *Interlocking Pattern.* This is also referred to as a *chain* or *circular story.* Each story scenario is connected to the one before in an interesting, reliable fashion. The plot is interlinked so that the ending leads back to the beginning.

5. *Chronological Pattern.* These stories follow a time sequence such as "Days of the Week" or "Numbers."

6. *Familiar Cultural Pattern.* Also referred to as *familiar sequence,* here the story pattern involves an easily recognizable sequence such as alphabet, numbers, days of the week, months of the year, seasons, and holidays.

7. *Problem-Centered Story.* Also referred to as the *problem-solution pattern* in that stories are structured around a dilemma with subsequent episodes leading to a resolution.

8. *Main Character.* The ideas of the story center around the main character who may be an animal or a human. For example, the well-known Curious George (Rey) stories are predictable because the readers come to know the main character, George, and the similar story lines and vocabulary associated with his adventures in these books.

In addition to the list above, Simpson (1986) suggests that the following fit the category of predictable text as well:

1. *Question and Answer.* The same or similar questions are repeated throughout the story.

2. *Songbooks.* Familiar songs with predictable features, such as repetitive lyrics, stanzas, or phrases.

The following list of predictable book selections has been adapted from Nellie Edge's website and V. Richey (1996).

1. Repetitive:

The same phrase, sentence, or story scenario repeats throughout the story.

Ask Mr. Bear	Flack
At Mary Bloom's	Aliki
Big Orange Splot	Pinkwater
Brown Bear, Brown Bear, What Do You See?	Martin
Caps for Sale	Slobodkina
Carrot Seed	Krauss
Caterpillar and the Polliwog	Kent
Chick and the Duckling	Ginsburg
Dance Away	Shannon
Dark, Dark Tale	Brown
Do You Know What I'll Do?	Zolotow
Doorbell Rang, The	Hutchins
Fortunately	Charlip
Going for a Walk	deRegniers
Good-night, Owl!	Hutchins
If I Found a Wistful Unicorn	Ashford
Important Book, The	Brown
It Looked Like Spilt Milk	Shaw
Jesse Bear, What Will You Wear?	Carlton
Jump, Frog, Jump	Kalan
King Bidgood's in the Bathtub	Wood
Klippity Klop	Emberley
Lizard's Song	Shannon
Love You Forever	Munsch
Mary Wore Her Red Dress	Peek
Millions of Cats	Gag
Mother, Mother, I Want Another	Polushkin
My Mom Travels a Lot	Bauer
Q is for Duck	Elting
Quick as a Cricket	Wood
Rain	Kalan
Roll Over	Gerstein
Sadie and the Snowman	Morgan
Someday	Zolotow
Three Billy Goats Gruff	traditional
Three Little Pigs	traditional
Very Busy Spider	Carle
Witch's Hat	Johnston
Who Sank the Boat?	Allen
Wonderful Shrinking Shirt	Anderson
That's Good, That's Bad	Cuyler

2. Cumulative:

Each time a new event occurs, all previous events in the story are repeated. In other words, each part repeats the previous part and then a new part is added.

Bringing the Rain to Kapiti Plain	Ardema
Elephant and the Bad Baby	Vipont
Enormous Turnip	Parkinson
Fat Cat: A Danish Folktale	Kent
Fiddle-i-fee	Stanley
Great Big Enormous Turnip	Oxenbury
Hairy MacClary from Donaldson's Dairy	Dodd
Henny Penny	Galdone
House That Jack Built	Stevens
I Know an Old Lady	traditional
Jacket I Wear in the Snow	Neitzel
Little Old Lady Who Was Not Afraid of Anything	Williams
Little Red Hen	Galdone
Napping House	Wood
No Jumping on the Bed	Arnold
"Not Me," Said the Monkey	West
Old Woman and Her Pig	Galdone
Over the Steamy Swamp	Geherety
Silly Sally	Wood
Teeny Tiny	Bennett
Too Much Noise	McGovern

3. Rhythm/Rhyme Sequence:

Rhyming words, refrains, or patterns are used and repeated throughout the story.

Brown Bear, Brown Bear, What Do You See?	Martin
Friendly Book	Brown
Good Night, Moon	Brown
I Like Bugs	Flanagan
Lady with the Alligator Purse	Westcott
Noisy Nora	Wells
Once a Lullaby	Nichol
Round is a Pancake	Sullivan
Seven Little Monsters	Sendak
Sitting on the Farm	King
Willy O'Dwyer Jumped in the Fire	deRegniers
Witch's Hat	Johnston

4. Interlocking Pattern:

This is also referred to as a *chain* or *circular story*. Each story scenario is connected to the one before in an interesting, reliable fashion. The plot is interlinked so that the ending leads back to the beginning.

Allison's Zinnia	Lobel
Blue Sea	Kalan
Chick and the Duckling	Ginsburg
Day Jimmy's Boa Ate the Wash	Noble
Each Pear Each Plum	Ahlbert
Five Chinese Brothers	Bishop
Gossip	Pienkowski
Happy Birthday, Dear Duck	Bunting
Hide and Snake	Baker
If You Give a Mouse a Cookie	Numeroff
If You Give a Moose a Muffin	Numeroff
Jump, Frog, Jump	Kalan
King, the Mice and the Cheese	Gurney
One Fine Day	Hogrogian
Mr. Willowby's Christmas Tree	Barry
Runaway Bunny	Brown
Willy O'Dwyer	deRegniers

5. Chronological Pattern:

These stories follow a time sequence such as "Days of the Week" and "Numbers."

Caterpillar and the Polliwog	Kent
Giving Tree	Silversteen
Go Tell Aunt Rhody	Aliki
Grouchy Ladybug	Carle
Growing Vegetable Soup	Ehlert
Love You Forever	Munsch
Papa, Please Get the Moon for Me	Carle
Red Leaf, Yellow Leaf	Ehlert
Sand Cake	Asch
Seasons of Arnold's Apple Tree	Gibbons
Sun's Day	Gerstein
Sun's Up	Euvremer
Very Hungry Caterpillar	Carle

6. Familiar Cultural Pattern:

Also referred to as *familiar sequence*, here the story pattern involves an easily recognizable sequence such as alphabet, numbers, days of the week, months of the year, seasons, and holidays.

Busy Monday Morning	Domanska
Chicken Soup with Rice	Sendak
Cookie's Week	Ward
Heckety Peg	Woods
May I Bring a Friend?	deRegniers
Over in the Meadow	Keats
Q is for Duck	Elting
Roll Over	Gerstein
Six Foolish Fishermen	Elkin
10 Bears in My Bed	Mack
Ten Little Caterpillars	Martin
This Old Man	Koontz
When Sheep Cannot Sleep	Kitamura

7. Problem-Centered Story:

Also referred to as the *problem-solution pattern* in that stories are structured around a dilemma with subsequent episodes leading to a resolution.

Curious George	Rey
Hansel and Gretel	traditional
Mean Soup	Everett
Millions of Cats	Gag
Rumplestiltskin	traditional
Thundercake	Polacco
Tikki Tikki Tembo	Mosel

8. Main Character:

The ideas of the story center around the main character who may be an animal or a human. For example, the well-known Curious George (Rey) stories are predictable because the readers come to know the main character, George, and the similar story lines and vocabulary associated with his adventures in these books.

Amelia Bedelia books	Parish
Anansi the Spider	Kimmel
Arthur books	Brown
Curious George books	Rey
Iktomi	Galdone
Magic School Bus	Cole

9. Question and Answer:

The same or similar questions are repeated throughout the story.

Black Crow, Black Crow	Fogelsong
Brown Bear, Brown Bear	Martin
Is It Time?	Janovitz
Where's My Share?	Greeley
Whose Footprints?	Coxe
Whose Mouse Are You?	Krause

10. Songbook:

Familiar songs with predictable features, such as repetitive lyrics, stanzas, or phrases.

The Farmer in the Dell	Zuromskis
The Green Grass Grows All Around	Hoffman
One Wide River To Cross	Emberly
Over on the Farm	Turner
Over in the Meadow	Keats
Over in the Meadow	Langstaff
Sitting on the Farm	King
Soldier, Soldier, Won't You Marry Me?	Langstaff

Nellie Edge also recommends "Favorite Books That Sing," some of which are listed here. The entire list may be found at: www.nellieedge.com/FavoriteBooksThatSing.htm.

America the Beautiful	Bates
Cumbayah	Cooper
Do Your Ears Hang Low?	Church
The Farmer in the Dell	Wallner
Frog Went A-Courtin'	Watson
Go Tell Aunt Rhody	Aliki
Head, Shoulders, Knees and Toes	Kubler
Hush Little Baby	Aliki
I Know an Old Lady	Bonne
Inch by Inch	Mallet
I've Been Working on the Railroad	Wescott
London Bridge is Falling Down	Spier
My Favorite Things	Graef
Old MacDonald Had a Farm	Wells
Over the River and Through the Woods	Turkle
She'll Be Comin' Round the Mountain	Coplon
Skip to My Lou	Westcott
The Star Spangled Banner	Spier
Take Me Out to the Ballgame	Norworth
This Land is Your Land	Guthrie
Twinkle, Twinkle Little Star	Hague
What a Wonderful World	Weiss and Thiele
Wheels on the Bus	Wickstrom
Yankee Doodle	Kellogg

Recommended Teacher Resource Books

Beck, I. L. (2006). *Making sense of phonics: The hows and whys.* New York: Guilford Press.

Blevins, W. (2006). *Phonics from A to Z: A practical guide.* New York: Scholastic.

Blevins, W. (2001). *Teaching phonics and word study in the intermediate grades: A complete sourcebook.* New York: Scholastic.

Campbell, R. (2004). *Phonics naturally: Reading and writing for real purposes.* Portsmouth, NH: Heinemann.

Cunningham, P. M., & Hall, D. P. (1994). *Making words: Multilevel, hands-on, developmentally appropriate spelling and phonics activities.* Carthage, IL: Good Apple.

Dahl, K. L., Scharer, P. L., Lawson, L. L., & Grogan, P. R. (2001). *Rethinking phonics: Making the best teaching decisions.* Portsmouth, NH: Heinemann.

Fox, B.J. (2008). *Word identification strategies: Building phonics into a classroom reading program.* Upper Saddle River, NJ: Pearson.

Fox, B. J. (2003). *Word recognition activities: Patterns and strategies for developing fluency.* Upper Saddle River, NJ: Merrill Prentice Hall.

Ganske, K. (2006). *Word sorts and more: Sound, pattern, and meaning explorations K–3.* New York: Guilford Press.

Gentry, J. R. (2006). *Breaking the code: The new science of beginning reading and writing.* Portsmouth, NH: Heinemann.

McLaughlin, M., & Fisher, L. (2005). *Research-based reading lessons for K–3.* New York: Scholastic.

Rasinski, T. V., & Padak, N. D. (2001). *From phonics to fluency: Effective teaching of decoding and reading fluency in the elementary school.* New York: Longman.

Rasinski, T. V., & Zimmerman, B. Z. (2001). *Phonics poetry: Teaching word families.* Boston: Allyn and Bacon.

Book Club Ideas

*T*hroughout the book, you have seen icons indicating activities or discussion points that lend themselves to book club conversations. We hope you and your colleagues will take advantage of these opportunities. Our experience has taught us that learning from and with each other is a powerful way to promote innovation. In this appendix, we provide additional questions and ideas for discussion. They are organized according to the chapters in the book.

Introduction: Phonics

- Look more closely at the report of the National Reading Panel. Make notes about key insights and the classroom implications of these insights. Share these with colleagues. (The report is available online at www.nationalreadingpanel.org. A shorter version is available at www.nifl.gov/partnershipforreading/publications/PFRbookletBW.pdf.)

- Select a piece of follow-up reading from the NRP website or at the National Institute for Literacy (http://nifl.gov). Make and share notes with your colleagues.

- Think back to the beginning of your teaching career. What were you taught about teaching phonics? Share these insights with your colleagues and together attempt to determine the major changes in the teaching of phonics over the course of your teaching careers as well as the research-based reasons for these changes.

Chapter 1: Phonics Instruction: What Does Research Tell Us?

- Make notes about the relationship among phonemic awareness, phonics, and reading achievement. With your colleagues, write a paragraph, based on scientific research, that explains this relationship.
- Talk with colleagues about what may account for children's difficulties in learning or using phonics. For each reason you can identify, make instructional plans for addressing it.
- Together with colleagues think about ways to tuck phonics instruction and practice into content area study.

Chapter 2: Instructional Strategies for Phonics Development

- Decide on two or three instructional strategies from this chapter that are new to you and that seem well suited to your instructional style. Explain to your colleagues why each is a good fit.
- For each strategy selected, make plans for implementation. Keep track of your questions as well and share these with colleagues.
- For each strategy selected, make plans to assess impact. That is, how will you determine if the addition of these strategies is having a positive influence on your students' phonics ability? Share your ideas with colleagues and invite their feedback.
- If you are currently using a commercial phonics program, evaluate it using the questions posed at the end of the chapter. If your evaluation identifies weaknesses, discuss these with your colleagues and make plans to strengthen these weak areas.

Chapter 3: Assessing Phonics Development

- Discuss each "big idea" in more detail. Decide if you agree or disagree with each, why, and what implications the ideas have for your classroom assessment plans for phonics.

- Complete the inverted triangle (page 46) with specific assessment plans for your students. Share your decisions with colleagues. Invite their feedback, particularly in regard to feasibility.

- List all possible revisions to your classroom assessment plans for phonics. Then rank order the items on the list. Explain your reasoning to your colleagues.

- For the most important revision idea from the activity above, develop an implementation plan. Share this with your colleagues and seek their feedback.

Chapter 4: Fostering Home-School Connections

- Develop detailed notes about the following: How do you currently explain phonics development and instruction to parents? What do you currently do to help parents see the role they can play to support their children's phonics learning?

- Review suggested phonics activities for the home. Select two or three that seem especially useful and feasible for your students. Make concrete plans for sharing these with parents. Include ELL families in your plans.

- Find out about agencies or programs in your area that offer English instruction for adults. Make connections with professionals in these agencies. Look for ways to partner with them such that parents and children can work together on phonics activities.

Chapter 5: Resources

- Review the lists of children's literature books offered in the chapter. Find and read several that you do not currently use. Make plans for incorporating these titles into instruction. Share your plans with colleagues.

- Explore one or two websites provided in the chapter. Make notes about possible classroom/home uses and share your ideas with colleagues.

- Search the Web for additional sites that can be useful for phonics instruction or practice in school or at home. Share what you find with colleagues.

Notes

*A*s you work through the book, you may want to make notes here about important ideas gleaned from discussions. You can keep track of additional resources. You may also want to use these pages to reflect on changes you made in your phonics instruction and to make notes about next steps.

General Issues and Ideas

Instructional Plans

_____

_____

_____

_____

_____

_____

_____

_____

_____

_____

_____

_____

_____

_____

_____

_____

_____

_____

_____

_____

_____

_____

_____

Notes

Notes

Assessment Plans

_____

_____

_____

_____

_____

_____

_____

_____

_____

_____

_____

_____

_____

_____

_____

_____

_____

_____

_____

_____

_____

_____

_____

Notes

APPENDIX B

Notes

Resources for Teachers

References

Adams, M. J. (1990). *Beginning to read: Thinking and learning about print.* Cambridge, MA: MIT Press.

Adler, R. (1985). Using closed-captioned television in the classroom. In L. Gambrell & E. McLaughlin (Eds.), *New directions in reading: Research and practice: Yearbook of the State of Maryland International Reading Association* (pp. 11–18). Silver Spring, MD: State of Maryland International Reading Association

Armbruster, B., & Osborn, J. (2001). *Put reading first: Research building blocks for teaching children to read.* Washington, DC: U.S. Department of Education.

Chiappe, P., Siegel, L. S., & Wade-Wooley, L. (2002). Linguistic diversity and the development of reading skills: A longitudinal study. *Scientific Studies of Reading, 6,* 369–400.

Bear, D., Invernizzi, M., Templeton, S., & Johnston, F. (2007). *Words their way* (4th ed.). Upper Saddle River, NJ: Prentice-Hall.

Beck, I. L. (2006). *Making sense of phonics: The hows and whys.* New York: Guilford Press.

Beck, I. L., & Juel, C. (1995 Summer). The role of decoding in learning to read. *American Educator, 8,* 21–25, 39–42.

Blevins, W. (2006). *Phonics from A to Z: A practical guide.* New York: Scholastic.

Burgess, S. R. (1999). The influence of speech perception, oral language ability, the home literacy environment, and prereading knowledge on the growth of phonological sensitivity: A 1-year longitudinal study. *Reading Research Quarterly, 34,* 400–402.

Calhoun, E. (2004). *Using data to assess your reading program.* Alexandria, VA: Association for Supervision and Curriculum Development.

Chall, J. (1983). *Stages of reading development.* New York: McGraw-Hill.

Chard, D. J., Pikulski, J. J., & McDonagh, S. H. (2006). Fluency: The link between decoding and comprehension for struggling readers. In T. Rasinski, C. Blachowicz, & K. Lems (Eds.), *Fluency instruction* (pp. 39–61). New York: Guilford Press.

Clay, M. (1993). *An observation survey of early literacy achievement.* Portsmouth, NH: Heinemann.

Clymer, T. (1963). The utility of phonics generalizations in the primary grades. *The Reading Teacher, 16,* 252–258.

Clymer, T. (1996). The utility of phonic generalizations in the primary grades. *The Reading Teacher, 50,* 182–187.

Cochrane, O. (1984). *Reading, writing, and caring.* New York: Richard C. Owens Publishers.

Cooter, R., Marrin, P., & Mills-House, E. (1999). Family and community involvement: The bedrock of reading success. *The Reading Teacher, 52,* 891–896.

Cunningham, A., & Stanovich, K. (1997). Early reading acquisition and its relation to reading experience and ability 10 years later. *Developmental Psychology, 33,* 934–945.

Cunningham, P. M. (1987). Action phonics. *The Reading Teacher, 41,* 247–249.

Cunningham, P. M., & Allington, R. L. (1994). *Classrooms that work: They can all read and write.* New York: HarperCollins.

Dahl, K. L., Scharer, P. L., Lawson, L. L., & Grogan, P. R. (2001). *Rethinking phonics: Making the best teaching decisions.* Portsmouth, NH: Heinemann.

Darling-Hammond, L., & McLaughlin, M. W. (1995). Policies that support professional development in an era of reform. *Phi Delta Kappan, 76,* 597–604.

Edge, N. *Favorite books that sing.* Retrieved July 18, 2007 from www .nellieedge.com/articles_resources/predictablebooks.htm.

Ehri, L. C. (1994). Development of the ability to read words: Update. In R. Ruddell, M. Ruddell, & H. Singer (Eds.), *Theoretical models and processes of reading* (pp. 323–358). Newark, DE: International Reading Association.

Fitzgerald J., & Graves, M. (2004). *Scaffolding reading experiences for English-language learners.* Norwood, MA: Christopher Gordon.

Fox, B. J. (2003). *Word recognition activities: Patterns and strategies for developing fluency.* Upper Saddle River, NJ: Merrill Prentice-Hall.

Fox, B. J. (2004). *Word identification strategies: Phonics from a new perspective* (3rd ed.). Upper Saddle River, NJ: Pearson Merrill Prentice-Hall.

Fox, B. J. (2008). *Word identification strategies: Building phonics into a classroom reading program.* Upper Saddle River, NJ: Pearson.

Fry, E. (1998). The most common phonograms. *The Reading Teacher, 51,* 620–622.

Gaskins, I., Ehri, L., Cress, C., O'Hara, C., & Donnelly, K. (1997). Procedures for word learning: Making discoveries about words. *The Reading Teacher, 50,* 312–327.

Gentry, J. R. (2006). *Breaking the code: The new science of beginning reading and writing.* Portsmouth, NH: Heinemann.

Gunn, B., Smolkowski, K., Biglan, A., & Black, C. (2002). Supplemental instruction in decoding skill for Hispanic and non-Hispanic students in early elementary school: A follow-up. *Journal of Special Education, 36,* 69–79.

Henderson, E. (1990). *Teaching spelling* (2nd ed.). Boston: Houghton Mifflin.

Henderson, E., & Beers, J. (Eds.). (1980). *Developmental and cognitive aspects of learning to spell.* Newark: DE: International Reading Association.

Johnston, F. R. (1999). The timing and teaching of word families. *The Reading Teacher, 53,* 64–75.

Juel, C., & Minden-Cupp, C. (2000). Learning to read words: Linguistic units and instructional strategies. *Reading Research Quarterly, 35,* 458–492.

Koskinen, P. S., et al. (1987). *Using the technology of closed-captioned television to teach reading to handicapped students.* Performance Report, United States Department of Education Grant No. G-00-84-30067. Falls Church, VA: National Captioning Institute.

Koskinen, P. S., Wilson, R. M., Gambrell, L. B., & Neuman, S. B. (1993). Captioned video and vocabulary learning: An innovative practice in literacy education. *The Reading Teacher, 47,* 36–43.

Lesaux, N. K., & Siegel, L. S.(2003). The development of reading in children who speak English as a second language. *Developmental Psychology, 39,* 1005–1019.

Lundberg, I. (1984, August). Learning to read. *School Research Newsletter.* Sweden: National Board of Education.

McCandliss, B., Beck, I. L., Sandak, R., & Perfetti, C. (2003). Focusing attention on decoding for children with poor reading skills: Design and preliminary tests of word building intervention. *Scientific Studies of Reading, 7,* 75–104.

McTighe, J., & Wiggins, G. (2004). *Understanding by design.* Alexandria, VA: Association for Supervision and Curriculum Development.

Moats, L. C. (1998). Teaching decoding. *American Educator, 22* (1 & 2), 42–49, 95.

Mraz, M., Gruhler, D., Padak, N., Peck, J., Kinner, J., McKeon, C., & Newton, E. (2001). Questions parents ask: The FAQ project. In W. Linek, E. Sturtevant, J. Dugan, & P. Linder (Eds.), *Celebrating the voices of literacy* (pp. 252–262). Readyville, TN: College Reading Association.

National Reading Panel. (2000). *Report of the National Reading Panel: Teaching children to read.* Report of the subgroups. Washington, DC: U.S. Department of Health and Human Services, National Institutes of Health.

Neuman, S. B., & Koskinen, P. S. (1992). Captioned television as comprehensible input: Effects of incidental word learning in context for language minority students. *Reading Research Quarterly, 27,* 95–106.

Pinnell, G. S., & Fountas, I. C. (2003). *Phonics lessons: Letters, words, and how they work.* Portsmouth, NH: Firsthand (an imprint of Heinemann).

Postlethwaite, T. N., & Ross, K. W. (1992). *Effective schools in reading: Implications for educational planners.* The Hague: International Association for Educational Achievement.

Rasinski, T. V., & Padak, N. D. (2001). *From phonics to fluency: Effective teaching of decoding and reading fluency in the elementary school.* New York: Longman.

Rasinski, T. V., & Padak, N. D. (2004). *Effective reading strategies: Teaching children who find reading difficult* (3rd ed.). Upper Saddle River, NJ: Pearson.

Rasinski, T. V., & Zimmerman, B. Z. (2001). *Phonics poetry: Teaching word families.* Boston: Allyn and Bacon.

Read, C. (1971). Pre-school children's knowledge of English phonology. *Harvard Educational Review, 41,* 1–34.

Read, C. (1975). *Children's categorization of speech sounds in English* (Research Report No. 17). Urbana, IL: National Council of Teachers of English.

Renyi, J. (1998). Building learning into the teaching job. *Educational Leadership, 55,* 5, 70–74.

Richey, V. (1996). *Kinds of predictable books.* Monroe County Public Library of Indiana. Retrieved July 18, 2007 from www.monroe.lib.in.us/childrens/predict.html.

Routman, R. (2003). *Reading essentials: The specifics you need to teach reading well.* Portsmouth, NH: Heinemann.

Routman, R., & Butler, A. (1995). Why talk about phonics? *School Talk, 1* (2). Urbana, IL: National Council Teachers of English.

Samuels, S. J. (2006). Reading fluency: Its past, present, and future. In T. Rasinski, C. Blachowicz, & K. Lems (Eds.), *Fluency instruction* (pp. 7–20). New York: Guilford Press.

Sénéchal, M., LeFevre, J., & Thomas, E. (1998). Differential effects of home literacy experiences on the development of oral and written language. *Reading Research Quarterly, 33,* 96–116.

Simpson, M. J. (1986). *Reading resource book: Parents and beginning reading.* Lakeworth, FL: Humanics Publishing Group.

Stahl, S. (1992). Saying the 'p' word: Nine guidelines for exemplary phonics instruction. *The Reading Teacher, 45,* 618–625.

Stanovich, K. (1986). Matthew effects in reading: Some consequences of individual differences in the acquisition of literacy. *Reading Research Quarterly, 21,* 360–407.

Stanovich, K. E., & West, R. F. (1989). Exposure to print and orthographic processing. *Reading Research Quarterly, 24*, 402–433.

Strickland, D. S. (1998). *Teaching phonics today: A primer for educators.* Newark, DE: International Reading Association.

Taylor, E., & Collins, V. (2003). *Literacy leadership for grades 5–12.* Alexandria, VA: Association for Supervision and Curriculum Development.

Tierney, R. (1998). Literacy assessment reform: Shifting beliefs, principled possibilities, and emerging practices. *The Reading Teacher, 51*, 374–390.

Tompkins, G. E. (2003). *Literacy for the 21st century: Teaching reading and writing in pre-kindergarten through grade 4.* Upper Saddle River, NJ: Merrill Prentice-Hall.

Trachtenburg, P. (1990). Using children's literature to enhance phonics instruction. *The Reading Teacher, 43*, 648–654.

Wang, C. C., & Gaffney, J. S. (1998). First graders' use of analogy in word recognition. *Journal of Literacy Research, 30*, 389–403.

Wenglinsky, H. (2000). *How teaching matters: Bringing the classroom back into discussions of teacher quality.* Princeton, NJ: Educational Testing Service.

West, K. (1998). Noticing and responding to learners: Literacy evaluation and instruction in the primary grades. *The Reading Teacher, 51*, 550–559.